In Search of
Ireland's Holy Wells

Elizabeth Healy

WOLFHOUND PRESS

Published in 2001 by
Wolfhound Press Ltd
68 Mountjoy Square
Dublin 1, Ireland
Tel: (353-1) 874 0354
Fax: (353-1) 872 0207

British Library Cataloguing in Publication Data
A catalogue record for this book is available from the British Library.

The publishers have made every reasonable effort to contact the copyright holders of material reproduced in this book. If any involuntary infringement of copyright has occurred, sincere apologies are offered and the owners of such copyright are requested to contact the publishers.

ISBN 0-86327-865-5

10 9 8 7 6 5 4 3 2 1

Except where otherwise stated, photographs in this book are by the author.

Quoted text, pages 95–96 © Pauric McGarvey, reproduced by kind permission.

'The Rag Tree, Boherard', from *News of the World: Selected Poems* (1998), reproduced by kind permission of *News of the World* and The Gallery Press.

Cover Photo: Image File
Typesetting and book design: Wolfhound Press
Printed in Spain by Edelvives

IN SEARCH OF
IRELAND'S HOLY WELLS

Detail from map prepared by John O'Donovan and included in James Hardiman's edition (1846) of *A Chorographic description of west or h-Iar Connaught* written in 1684 by Roderick O'Flaherty. The prevalence of holy wells can be judged from the large number of 'tobars' marked in the small area of country near Loughs Mask and Corrib.

Contents

To the many friends
who tolerated my enthusiasms and/or
accompanied me on my ramblings

Introduction

It started as a mere diversionary measure. Travelling can be tedious, and it is always nice to have a secondary objective to expand the interest of the journey, 'to shorten the road' so to speak, though in practice usually lengthening it considerably. From time to time my diversions have led me far off my intended route in favour of such things as old castles, round towers, megalithic tombs and standing stones. While none of these have lost their appeal, at some stage those wells or springs which have come to be known as holy wells got added to the list. And I got hooked.

The more of them I found, the more I became charmed by their great variety and also, very often, by the beauty of their location and form. As my fascination with them grew, they shifted status to primary objective and I started travelling to find them for their own sakes and, where possible, to attend on what is known as Pattern (or Patron) Day, the day of special devotion at any particular well.

St Declan's Well, Ardmore, County Waterford is located about ½ km east of the round tower and was traditionally visited on 24 July.

This was not always easy because, even where Patterns are still held, they are not always held on the traditional day but on a day which is regarded as more convenient, for instance a Sunday. In some cases, the day would be changed so as not to coincide with a sporting event or other special occasion. Also, as many of the Patterns fall on the same day, for instance the last Sunday of July or Garland Sunday, it would take several years to catch up on just a few. But they are many and varied enough to be worth the wait. Listening to me talk about my latest 'discoveries', and probably bored thereby, friends persuaded me to 'write a book about them'. After much nagging, I gave in.

This small book, then, is not in any sense an attempt to write about all of the holy wells in Ireland – an impossible task anyway, considering that there are literally thousands of them. It is intended just to give a flavour of the wide range of those still surviving, selected almost at random from those I have visited myself, and which for me have special appeal because of their form or their background story. I have not dealt, for instance, with such important and popular pilgrimage sites as Clonmacnois on the Shannon, that loveliest of holy places where prayers at St Ciarán's Well are 'part of the order to be followed by pilgrims in accordance with ancient custom'; with St Gobnait's, much-loved saint of Ballyvourney, County Cork, where an elaborate 'round' is attached to a monastic complex; Tobar na Molt, The Well of the Wethers near Ardfert in Kerry, where St Brendan the Navigator was baptised, and where people still gather on the Saturday before midsummer, though nobody now uses the little 'dressing house' which enabled people to bathe in the well to cure their rheumatism. There were numerous smaller, more hidden ones that had me trailing down byways, scrambling over ditches, fighting my way through bramble entanglements or over flowery embankments, pausing along the way maybe to pick wild strawberries.

There can hardly be a townland in Ireland that does not have at least one well or spring that by tradition is sacred or holy. Every reader has at least one in close proximity to where he or she lives. A great many are marked on the *Discovery* series of maps (scale 1:50,000) issued by the Ordnance Survey of Ireland. Searching them out is both a happy and rewarding experience and may even prompt the discoverer to 'adopt' a well and care for it if it appears to be in danger of becoming forgotten or neglected.

The wonder is that such fragile and vulnerable features of our landscape have survived through the centuries. This book is also, then, a plea for the cherishing of these links with the past. Attendance at the sacred springs is our oldest heritage. We should not let it die.

1

The Pattern at the Well

It is a glorious morning. The midwinter sun shines from an intensely blue sky. The last of the frost has melted underfoot. Ahead, the land falls off in a series of rocky bracken- and heather-clad shelves to the Atlantic, and a scattering of islands range themselves in the glittering sea.

Close by, a handful of people silently circle a small well among the rocks and grass. A collection of boots and shoes stands by the stone wall, inside a little gate. Bare feet scuff the wet grass and carefully negotiate the rocks. Around and around they circle, some kneel, a pebble is dropped here, and there. Heads stoop to drink from the well, and water is perhaps touched to eyes or throat. Then feet are washed in a rushy pool and footwear retrieved.

All the time little groups of people come and go, as they have done since midnight, and will until midnight tonight. Old friends meet on the way, quiet greetings are exchanged, friendships revived.

It is the annual 'Pattern', or Patron day, of a local 'saint' who may, or may not, be listed in the official canon. He is greatly venerated here, and no one living in the locality would miss coming to pay their respects to their beloved saint in the traditional manner on this day. This is a fishing community, and boats will go to sea with a bottle of water from the saint's well, to keep them safe from harm.

Removing my shoes, I follow the particular 'station' prescribed for this well. The word station is used to refer both to the prescribed ritual and also to each of the features associated with the well, in this case two circular 'beds' or mounds of stones. The station is engraved on a plaque, together with the admonishment that the station is usually done in bare feet.

Kneel at first station
Say a prayer
And pick up seven stones
Walk around the mound seven times
dropping a stone and saying
the Our Father, Hail Mary
and Glory each time around
Repeat at well
Leave something
That you brought with you
At the well
A coin stone or medal etc
Wash your feet in the pool
Beside the well
Take three sips of water from the well.

'Walk around the mound seven times ... dropping a stone each time around.' The age-old ritual is carried out by custom in bare feet. A bottle of water from the well will accompany fishing boats going to sea.

Finishing the station I retrieve my shoes. Then, careless, I slip on the sloping rock which has been smoothed by generations of circling feet. The shin is scraped, drawing blood. Immediately there is a circle of concerned faces and hands. I am helped to my feet, water from the well is poured over the wound, I am persuaded to drink a little of the well water. I go on my way with many good wishes and a small bottle of water which has been put into my hands. The wound heals in three days.

❧

Here at the beginning of the third millennium water still maintains its sacred significance. Our very survival depends on it. It is, after all, the essence of life. As a

'... take three sips of water ...'

Opposite page: St Colman's near Kinvara, County Galway.

human species we emerged from water, from ancient seas. We ourselves are largely made up of water and the water in our cells responds to the pull of the planets. We can last without food for many weeks, but without water we die in days. All the great civilisations of the world have arisen where there is water. Wars are still fought for control of water. Small wonder then that it is not only our bodies that respond to its power, but also our imaginations and even our souls.

Water cults have been universal throughout time and rituals associated with water still take place all over the world. The great sacred rivers, the Nile and the Ganges, have rituals associated with the whole life cycle of the peoples who live along their pathways. In every culture traditional water rites can be found — from such important rites as those for rain-making, for flood-prevention, for healing, for fertility, down to such simple practices as bathing our faces in the dew of May mornings.

There is something deeply moving in seeing water, especially pure spring water, gush forth from the ground — as an offering from the earth itself or, as the ancients would have said, from the mother earth goddess. Well-worship was prevalent in pre-Christian Celtic cultures and, as far as western Europe is concerned, the survival of the practice is more noticeable in Ireland than elsewhere. But for all we know the practice may have already been old when the first wave of Celtic people arrived at our shores. There are holy wells close to many of the ancient, pre-Celtic sites. Why should the emergence of pure water from the earth have had less sacred significance to the stone-age hunters and gatherers, who were the first arrivals after the ice sheets withdrew from the mountains, than to their successors?

When Christianity came, it was only natural that churches would be built on sites that were already sacred. The associated wells would have been blessed and assimilated into the new religion and the cult practices adapted to give new meaning.

2

Why 'Holy'?

So, what then makes a holy well holy? A simple answer is to say that, usually, it is a well or spring dedicated to a saint, around which some religious or cult-type activity has arisen. But, a holy well does not always have a saint's name attached, and when account is taken of such diversity as saint's wells, pin wells, rag wells, healing wells and wells with specialities such as wart wells and eye wells, we see that the variety is enormous. Many of them carry with them the signs of their pre-Christian origin. As to old deities, what could be more direct an association with gods and goddesses than the well dedicated to Crobhderg, a pagan deity, at the place called The City, just north of the twin mountains known as The Paps of Dana, or Anu, in Kerry? 'Rounds' are still made there, and cattle were driven around the well on May Day until fear of bovine diseases put a stop to the practice in modern times. By assimilating such cultic places, the new Christian churches helped to preserve them into our own time.

Votive offerings on *Weepers'* altar, *Tobar na Molt* or *Well of the Wethers*, near Ardfert, County Kerry. The well is dedicated to St Brendan the Navigator and is visited especially on the Saturday before midsummer.

Photo: Roinn Bhéaloideas Éireann

Wells are visited for different reasons, for favours or cures, for penance or thanksgiving, and sometimes purely out of piety and respect for the saint to whom the well is dedicated. They are visited by individuals at any time, but traditionally there was a special day, usually but by no means always the feast day of the saint — the Pattern or Patron Day, on which large crowds would gather, and still do in many cases. The Celtic year was divided into four seasons: Imbolc, spring, beginning on 1 February; Bealtaine, or May-day, the beginning of summertime; Lughnasa, named after the great god Lugh, the harvest festival at the end of July or beginning of August, and Samhain, 1 November. They represented birth, growth, fruitfulness and death, and each carried its own celebration. A large number of Patterns, particularly those relating to mountain sites, still take place at the time of the old Lughnasa feast, now usually celebrated on the last Sunday of July, which is also known as Garland Sunday.

In the past the religious or quasi-religious practices would be followed by sporting events, music and dancing and general merrymaking that went on late into the night. These celebrations led, as often as not, to drunkenness and fighting, and for that reason they were frowned on by authority.

Up to 3,000 holy wells have been recorded in Ireland. Many of them will by now have been abandoned or forgotten, and if not altogether lost, so neglected as to make them difficult to locate. More surprising, perhaps, is the fact that so many of them are still 'active' in the sense that they are still visited and that there are quite a few of them whose Pattern day is still celebrated. Furthermore, a large number that had faded into insignificance, or that had retained only a small number of faithful devotees, are being 'resurrected', and newly incorporated into contemporary religious practices and ceremonies led by the local Parish Priest or even, in some cases, by the local Bishop.

Sketch taken at Ronogue's Well, near Cork by D. Maclise, for *Barrow's Tour Round Ireland.*
Courtesy the National Library of Ireland

This is particularly pleasing as, during the eighteenth and nineteenth centuries in particular, both the civil and ecclesiastical authorities made considerable attempts to discourage attendance at the wells and at the celebrations that followed.

My own first contact with a holy well was in Crosshaven, County Cork, where as children we spent the long summers. It was not called a 'holy well' then; even as long ago as that it had lost its real meaning, but it was regarded nonetheless with unease and some apprehension. We were told to 'stay away from it', which, of course, increased its fascination for us. I went looking for it recently. At first I thought it had disappeared, or that my memory was deceiving me. I had to enquire of a passer-by who, after a little thought, seemed to remember and pointed me towards a stile in a new wall, leading to a wood that became familiar as I approached it.

I followed, where I could distinguish it, the old, indistinct track through the woods. Finally, parting a particularly dense entanglement of briars and willow scrub, I found it. It was not lost at all, and although overgrown with ferns and marsh marigold,

St Ciarán's Well at Clonmacnois, County Offaly. The well lies outside the monastic complex but is visited as part of the 'Long Station' or pilgrimage rite.

its little protecting wall of stones was still intact, and the water bubbling up was clear and sparkling. It ran along to lose itself in thicker scrub among the trees, where I could not follow it.

I was childishly pleased, not only because it brought back memories of what always seemed to be long sunny days of perfect happiness, but that it had not been forgotten, even though there were no signs of recent visitors.

I have spent many happy days searching out holy wells, not only the well-known and 'national' ones, which, of course, are interesting, but with even greater affection and pleasure the little wells of purely local veneration. They have led me into some of the loveliest parts of hidden Ireland, deeply rural landscapes where often the loudest noise is the lowing of cows and the calling of thrushes. I have often found myself in a haze of delight, wandering forgotten laneways fringed with Queen Anne's Lace or under arches of ancient trees, at times when the countryside is drowned under a froth of May blossom and the air full of the scent of gorse or meadowsweet.

But holy wells are not just confined to the countryside. Even Dublin City has its share.

Opposite page: *The Holy Well* by William Orpen (1878–1931), is heroic and highly imaginative. It hangs now in the National Gallery of Ireland, Dublin.
By kind permission of the William Orpen Estate and The National Gallery of Ireland

3

Wells in the Capital

The Ordnance Survey Office records one hundred and eighteen holy wells in the county of Dublin alone, several of them within what are now the city boundaries. As you walk along Nassau Street, past the entrance to Trinity College, there is one beneath your feet. It is railed off now, for reasons of safety or security, but any of the groundsmen in Trinity can be persuaded to bring you to its large entrance under the street. It is dedicated to St Patrick who is said to have brought it into being as a sweet well when the local denizens complained to him that the local water was brackish. In Drumcondra there is St Catherine's Well which has a cure for toothache, St Fintan's Well in Sutton has a cure for eye and stomach disorders, St Donogh's Well in Upper Kilbarrack 'was formerly held in great estimation for the curing of all disorders for which purpose it was much frequented'. And so on.

The city suburbs have now spread out in a tidal wave to inundate a vast area of what was until recently meadows and wheat fields. Lady's Well in Mulhuddart was for centuries a famous well, and its Pattern Day, 8 September, a big occasion for the surrounding countryside. It is to be found on a narrow stretch of old road that (at time of writing) still survives among the new housing estates, across from the remnants of a church dedicated to the Virgin Mary. Around 1740 a traveller, one Isaac Butler, wrote that:

About midway ascending to ye Church is an excellent Well; it is carefully walled, and several large trees about it. Here on the 8 September, a great patron is kept with a vast Concourse of all Sexes and Ages from many miles, upwards of eighty Tents are pitched here furnished with all kinds of Liquors and provisions for ye Reception and Refreshment of ye Company.

The 'all kinds of Liquors and provisions' appear, however, to have led to too much merriment over the years, with the result that this notice appeared in Faulkner's *Dublin Journal* of 15 August 1754:

We are assured that the Roman Catholic Clergy to prevent as far as in them lieth, the enormities and scandalous excesses that are annually committed at the Well near Mulahedard, commonly called Lady's Well, have prevailed on the landholders contiguous thereto not to permit any tents or booths to be erected hereafter upon any part of their lands; of which it is judged proper to give notice in this publick manner, to prevent a disappointment to such publicans as usually erected tents or booths near said Well.

Considering that the houses are relentlessly advancing across the fields to it, and that children swinging on the 'large trees' (which are so old-looking one could imagine them to be the same ones mentioned in 1740) know nothing about it, the well is in remarkably good repair, and despite the rubbish which regularly accumulates inside it, the water still runs clear. The children were astonished when asked whether they ever saw anyone praying there, but one of them said he thought 'a healer came there sometimes' but didn't know when.

The spring is on the side of the road having, according to legend, moved across the road when attempts were made to stop it. It is covered by a roofed masonry structure about 120 centimetres (four foot) high with an opening at each end, like a miniature oratory. The custom was for the pilgrim to lie on the ground and put his or her head in one of the openings to drink. As the disapproving Isaac Butler describes the practice: 'there's a hole in each end – the people lye on their bellies there with their head over the water repeat a prayer and drink and repeat another prayer before the little glazed bauble'. The 'glazed bauble' would have been a statue in a niche by the roof. The water was reputed to have a cure for sprains, cuts and bruises and rheumatism. A local woman claims a cure in

three days for a child who had a rash all over her body for which the doctors had no cure.

Lady's Well, Mulhuddart, County Dublin. This well looks exactly the same as it did a century ago, except for the houses in the background. The custom was for pilgrims to lie on their stomachs and drink the water through the opening. It is said to have a cure especially for sore eyes.

26

It has been kept in good repair by a number of local people, most recently by Andy Durrans. From time to time, depending on local clergy, devotions have been taking place at the well on 15 August, though people still visit it on the traditional day, which is 8 September.

Not far away from Lady's Well, at Diswellstown, is the site of what was once a very popular healing well known as the 'Rag Well'. This one is unusual in that not only was it a healing well, but it also supplied water to the neighbouring families for ordinary household purposes. It is claimed that it was the only well in the district that never ran dry. However, the County Council, in its wisdom, at some stage attached a pump to the well, from which indignity it never recovered and it eventually dried up. A little flowerbed marks the spot now, with an inscription 'Rag Well' on the wall above it.

Rituals were carried out here in living memory, particularly on May Eve. The practice was to place lighted candles at the well, then to walk around it saying the Rosary. Those with eye problems would bathe the eyes with a rag, and leave the rag at the well, usually tied to a tree. The tree, sadly, has disappeared along with the healing water.

There is a holy well dedicated to St Brigid at a busy corner of Castleknock village, at the junction of the Chapelizod Road. This also was covered over and a pump attached, which doesn't seem to operate any more. But the tradition of the place is at least acknowledged by a modern sheltering wall of brick, supporting two stones with the inscriptions: 'Jesus said whosoever drinketh of this water shall thirst again but whosoever drinketh of the water I shall give him shall never thirst. John IV Chap. 14 Verse.' and 'He (Jesus) shall lead them into living fountains of water: and God shall wipe away all tears from their eyes. Revelations Vll Chap 17 Verse.'

Many of these practices, especially the one at Lady's Well of lying on the stomach and putting the head inside to drink, were the remnants of pre-Christian practices. This brings us to St Brigid, to whom so many holy wells throughout the country are dedicated.

St Brigid's Well near Kildare town. The photograph was taken on 1 February and the candles from the previous evening's vigil can be seen.

4

When Spring Begins

In Ireland, we know St Brigid (Brighid, Brigit or Bridget) as 'Mary of the Gael', 'the Fiery Arrow', second only to Patrick in the hierarchy of patron saints. Her feast day, the first day of February, heralds in the spring. She was bountiful and generous. She was a great dairywoman, and her ale was as famous as her charity. Flames of fire appeared to come from any house in which she slept. She was the daughter of a slave, fathered by the chieftain Dubhtach. Mother and daughter were banished by Dubhtach's jealous wife until Brigid was reclaimed by the chief. Her energy and talents won freedom for both herself and her mother. She eventually established a community of women at Kildare which became a centre for crafts and manuscripts. She later founded a monastery, and acquired great political power. A perpetual fire blazed at her headquarters. Her miracles were legion. That is our Brigid, patron saint.

Long before our Christian saint, there was Brigid ('the exalted one'), Celtic goddess

There are wells dedicated to St Brigid all over Ireland. This one, which has been much restored, is close to Mullingar, County Westmeath.

of Fertility, venerated in Gaul and Britain and probably more widely in Continental Europe. She was daughter of Daghda, the chief god of the Celts (the equivalent of the Roman Saturn) and her responsibilities were livestock, the dairy, the home, poetry, traditional learning and sacred wells. The goddess Brigid was a Triad: the Brigid of Poetry, the Brigid of Healing and the Brigid of Smithcraft. Her healing powers were exercised largely through poetic incantation at sacred wells.

Because Kildare is Cill Dara, the Church of the Oak Tree, and the oak was the sacred tree of the Druids, it is suggested[1] that there already existed a pagan sanctuary at Kildare which was Christianised by a holy woman of the Fothartha (Dubhthach's tribe). Thus the name of the Brigid-goddess and the cult of the sanctuary, including its sacred well, would have become attached to her. The fact that St Brigid's Day falls on 1 February, the old pagan feast of Imbolc which signals the onset of spring, emphasises the fertility theme. She was associated with birth, growth and fruitfulness.

I should like a lake of ale for the King of
    Kings
I should like the household of heaven to
    be there drinking it for eternity
I should like cheerfulness to be in the
    drinking
I should like Jesus here also.

Brigid is the perfect example of the synthesis of pagan and Christian, a process which has applied across many rites and practices, and in particular to what were the sacred wells of the Celts. How her attributes changed from those of fertility to those of chastity is an interesting insight into social history.

The Christian Brigid, no doubt like her predecessor, acquired such a powerful image that there are wells dedicated to her all over

---

1. Ó hÓgáin, Daithí, *Myth, Legend & Romance* (Prentice Hall, 1991).

Ireland. The most important ones are at Faughart in County Louth, her birthplace according to legend, and at Kildare where she established her monastery and where she is one of the patrons of the diocese. The story of how she came by the land to build her monastery is well known throughout Ireland; the local chieftain cynically offered her only as much land as her cloak would cover, but when the cloak was laid on the ground, it spread to cover an area so big that the chieftain had to beg her to stop before he lost all his territory.

All wells dedicated to St Brigid are visited on 1 February. At Kildare there are elaborate celebrations organised by a group which includes the Brigidine Sisters. The celebrations are now part of a two-day event and are incorporated into a seminar dealing with wider issues of justice and care for the environment. They are a new perspective on age-old Brigidine concerns and rituals, part of the unbroken tradition of veneration long pre-dating our Christian saint. One of the rituals re-introduced by the Sisters is the lighting of St Brigid's Flame on the eve of the feast, which they do in the centre of the town.

There are in fact two venerated wells, both on the edge of the town. There is 'the wayside well' in a semicircular alcove close to the car park of the Japanese Gardens, which is thought to have the pre-Christian connection. Although it was always visited by individuals, public rituals stopped taking place there because of its position close to a curve on the road where increasing traffic made it dangerous. When I visited there some years ago on a February morning, there was a little jar of snowdrops and the remains of two candles, left by someone faithful to the oldest site. In recent times, however, work has been done to create easier access. It has been nicely landscaped and is regaining some of its old popularity.

The major rituals have for several years been taking place at the other well, at nearby Tully. Here the water from the spring runs through a channel which is interrupted halfway along by two holed stones through which the water flows. The suggestion is that these represent the breasts of the saint,

Opposite page and right: St Brigid's Well, Liscannor, County Clare. The countless votive offerings lining the walls of the passage to the well are a strangely potent testament to decades of faith and devotion.

incorporating symbols of her fertility and her association with milk. Present-day rituals include a candle-lit procession and bonfire on the eve of the feast day, rosaries and other prayers and hymn-singing on the following morning. The traditional 'rounds' appear to have been substituted by the procession, the candles and the leaving of apples, but the taking of water from the well is still a feature. The ancient goddess may appear to have been forgotten, but she has merely been subsumed into an elaborate modern celebration which could be quite appropriately described as 'Celtic Christianity'.

The well that is probably the most visited in Ireland in these modern times is St Brigid's Well at Liscannor, County Clare. It is not devout pilgrims or troubled petitioners, however, that form the bulk of the visitors, but tourists. The well is on the main route to the famed Cliffs of Moher, and every coach stops and disgorges its occupants to view the curiosity with little or no understanding of its significance.

This is a pity, because it is a very beautiful and deeply moving place, where generations of Irish people brought their sorrows and ailments, their fears and needs, leaving behind some token to remind the Saint or, before that, the local god of their petition of grief or gratitude.

St Brigid's Well lies by the roadside, on the slopes above the sea between Liscannor Bay and the Cliffs. Dr Máire MacNeill in her wonderful book *The Festival of Lughnasa* describes this well as 'one of the three most strongly lasting survivals of Lughnasa', the other two being the Croagh Patrick pilgrimage in Mayo and the bacchanalian romp that is Puck Fair in Kerry. What is now to be seen at Liscannor is a large newly landscaped walled area with a gravelled garden and a central mound surmounted by a statue of St Brigid. The gravelled garden is in stark contrast to the well enclosure itself which thankfully has not been disturbed. The well is at the back of a deep cavernous passage, where the water falls in a thin stream into a square rock basin. An

St Brigid's Well at Killare, County Westmeath is overlooked by the historic Hill of Uisneach.

astonishing array of pious mementoes crowd the walls of the passage — statues of Brigid and other saints, some dressed in cloth and silvery veils. There are the usual 'holy pictures', coins, rosaries, ribbons and so on, but also handwritten notes, requests for prayers for sick relatives or other needs; there are a few crutches and burning candles, all tokens of favours asked or in gratitude for favours received.

The Pattern was traditionally attended in huge numbers from the surrounding area. The custom was to arrive at the well before nightfall on the eve and remain there throughout the night, performing the traditional rounds with their repeated prayers. Most of the congregation then repaired to the beach at Lahinch three miles away for a day of races and other sports on the strand, ending with dancing, music and merriment. It was a particularly popular occasion with the Aran Islanders, who used to come in great numbers. They would come in currachs from Inisheer via Doolin and walk the five miles to Liscannor, to arrive before nightfall. They would stay around the well all night, 'singing sweetly until the light of day came on them'. Many people came just to hear the islanders singing. Such crowds no longer celebrate Lughnasa or Garland Sunday and the races and sports on the beach are no longer an event. Few now come to make the vigil. Those who do are more inclined to come alone, or in small groups, on St Brigid's Day, or on 15 August, the Feast of the Assumption.

While I was there on a June day, two coaches full of tourists stopped, the fifty or

Opposite page: One of the forty or more holy wells in the mostly waterless Burren of County Clare, this one high on the 'green road' leading south-west from Formoyle. It has a cure for toothache and sore eyes, though the 'House Blessing' prayer and the shoe suggest that other troubles are brought to the well.

so occupants alighted, looked around curiously, went inside the well passage and took photographs. After they had departed a rather large car drove up. A smartly-dressed woman stepped out, scooped out some water from the well, poured it over her bared foot (I could see a bandaged toe), blessed herself, said a prayer and went off cheerfully.

Steps beside the well enclosure lead up to an old graveyard where an obelisk tops the tomb of Cornelius O'Brien, nineteenth-century landlord and local Member of Parliament. A much taller obelisk a short distance away, erected by the same man in 1853 (at the expense of his reluctant tenants) shortly before he died, is known locally as 'Cornelius O'Brien's last erection'.

The sheer quantity and variety of votive offerings and pious mementoes at this St Brigid's Well is probably unique in Ireland, but the custom of leaving such objects is widespread. They are to be found at almost every holy well in Ireland. The petitioners leave a reminder of their needs, something to continue the petition, like a prayer wheel. Common objects are medals, coins, pins or buttons, but the variety is endless. If an ailment is the trouble, a rag or ribbon touched to the ailing part of the body is left. I have seen printed prayers, rosary beads, brooches, ribbons, pieces torn from garments, small statues of the saint or the Blessed Virgin, holy pictures, prayer books, handwritten appeals, babies' shoes or even soothers. They represent the fears and sufferings brought to the well, the hardships endured through centuries of poverty and strife, of illness, of the fear of barrenness. And now, in times of greater ease and prosperity, have we no needs? Indications are otherwise.

Sometimes, of course, offerings are left in thanksgiving for favours received or problems solved, confirming the efficacy of the well.

Further north in County Clare, the strangely beautiful stone desert of the Burren sifts rainwater down through its limestone crevices, leaving on the surface one puny river and a few lakes that appear and disappear from time to time. Here, it could be thought that any well at all that holds water would be miraculous. However, over forty blessed wells have been listed, though none of these is dedicated to Brigid. Each of them is worth searching out among those 'little fields with boulders dotted, grey-stone shoulders saffron-spotted'.[2] Most beautiful to me is St Colman's (McDuach) Well, situated above the Early Christian churches at Oughtmama not far from Corcomroe Abbey, and Tobar Colman McDuach, tucked in under the cliffs of Slievecarron. St Colman's Well's special day is 5 November and it was regarded as being especially beneficial to eye troubles. It sits on the bare slopes above the graceful old abbey ruins. A rough stone wall surrounds it and an ash tree bends protectively over it.

It is a place to sit for hours looking over the magical grey and purple landscape, listening to the silence. Tobar Colman McDuach is by the hermitage where, the legend tells, the saint spent seven years in prayer and fasting. After his fast was ended, he prayed for sustenance. At that moment his kinsman, King Guaire, sitting to a meal in his castle, Dún Guaire near Kinvara, wished that the meal could be shared with someone hungry, at which point the entire meal was carried through the air to the saint's hermitage. You can just make out 'Bóthar na Miasa', the road of the dishes, to prove it!

The remnants of the hermitage and the well are difficult to locate now as the hazel scrub is gradually throwing a mantle over them, but the reward is the discovery of a place that lifts the heart and inspires the soul.

---

2. John Betjeman, *Ireland with Emily*.

5

The Hawk's Well?

You can, it may be,

Lead me to what I seek, a well wherein

Three hazels drop their nuts and
*   withered leaves,*

And where a solitary girl keeps watch

Among grey boulders. He who drinks,
*   they say,*

Of that miraculous water lives for ever.

In W.B. Yeats' play, *At The Hawk's Well*, an old man has spent his whole life by the magical well, waiting for the brief and sudden rush of water that will make him immortal. Each time the splash comes, the guardian spirit of the well has distracted his attention, and he misses the chance.

Tullaghan Well is deep in Yeats Country on the border of counties Sligo and Leitrim. Hawks used to come whirling and screaming from their eyrie on Hawk's Rock close by. Almost certainly it is the well that inspired the play.

The well is situated close to the summit of the modest hill called Tullaghan at the north-east end of the Ox Mountains. It offers a wide view of a storied landscape made familiar by the poet, from the hill of Knocknarea, under the cairn on whose summit 'passionate Maeve lies stony still', to Ballysodare Bay and its wide and beautiful strand. Tullaghan boasts three prehistoric cashels or ring-forts, one of which encloses most of the summit. This, added to the legends, would indicate a pre-Christian origin for rites at the well, which were always by tradition celebrated on Garland Sunday, or Lughnasa.

This well was counted among the *Mirabilia Hiberniae*, the Wonders of Ireland, by various early chroniclers. Many ancient sources document the 'fact' that the waters in the well ebbed and flowed according to the state of the tide in the sea beyond, and that the water was salt and fresh alternately. It seems that the water mark left by the subsided water was clear. It also held two magical trout, which were rarely seen. It was a magical well indeed, to hold water at all in that situation, so close to the hilltop.

Although it obviously dates from ancient times, in folklore its origin is attributed to St Patrick who banished the demons (it is not only snakes that merited his attention) from Croagh Patrick. But one of them, the Caorthannach, or the Devil's Mother, polluted all the wells along the path of her flight as he chased across the country to Tullaghan. By the time Patrick reached the hill he was parched and prayed for a drink, and a sweet well sprang up beside him.

A great Pattern was held up to the early nineteenth century, at which point a dramatic episode led to its demise, though individuals have continued to visit the well right into modern times. As with many such venues, visits to the well were only part of a festive day which continued into the night with sports, dancing, general merriment and usually a considerable amount of drunkenness, leading to faction fighting. Faction fights were regarded as a sport and usually no great harm came from them, but combined with drunkenness, they could lead to serious injuries or, occasionally, death.

At Tullaghan, as in Liscannor, it was the custom that, after devotions at the well, the action moved to the strand below. The State disapproved of the religious rites and, by an Act of Queen Anne, imposed fines or whippings on persons attending pilgrimages at holy wells, but it had no objections to the sports that accompanied them. The Church, on the other hand, encouraged piety at the well but frowned on the festivities on the strand. After the usual well rituals on the appointed day in 1826 greater crowds than ever assembled at the strand. Because it was a gloriously sunny day, it was believed that Providence approved of their customary entertainments in defiance of the clergy.

A contemporary account sets the scene:[1]

The tents were full of guzzlers; the itinerant dealers sold out their poteen and ginger-bread as fast as they could receive the price; dancing circles whirled here and there around pipers and fiddlers; ballad singers, unused as yet to the stirring patriotic productions of the modern national muse, drawled out their doleful ditties on highway robbery and murder; mountebanks, sleight-of-hand men, and cardsharpers performed their feats and tricks so as to engross the attention of the gaping rustic, while their accomplices, the pickpockets, plied the practised finger in his pockets; drunken men staggered and shouted, and flourished their shillelaghs; excited men moved about in knots and groups preparing for the fight of the night, which to them seemed the most interesting part of the patron; and, in a word, the whole Strand was a scene of riot and revelling, and a very Babel of noises, when, on a sudden, a pitch dark cloud overspread the sky, to which all eyes were instinctively directed.

A violent storm broke suddenly over the gathering, lightning flashed and thunder rolled, and rain came in torrents. The storm lasted all through the night, terrifying the

---

1.   Archdeacon O'Rorke in his *History of the Parish of Ballysodare*.

The Well of the Saints by J.M. Synge, as produced by the Abbey Theatre. The old couple are cured of their blindness, but discover that sight is not always to their advantage. *Photo: Amelia Stein*

people, many of whom regarded it as a judgement sent for defying their clergy.

The patron was never since revived; and thus was brought to a close, by what seemed to the people a direct interposition of Providence, a celebrated festive meeting which, partly on the Strand, but principally on Tullaghan hill, had been annually held for probably more than two thousand years, which had often brought with it disorders and bloodshed, and which had survived the most strenuous efforts to suppress it both of Church and State.

It is a sad fact that on my last visit, in May 1999, this lovely location was almost totally inaccessible, not only because no right-of-way appears to have been maintained across private land, but because the hill was totally overgrown with impenetrable brambles, a condition which had developed over a short number of years.

J.M. Synge also had his holy-well play, *The Well of the Saints.* It was on his first visit to the Aran Islands off County Galway that Synge became interested in the theme of a miraculous cure for blindness, on hearing a story about a blind boy whose sight had been restored at the holy well near the old ruined church of the *Ceathair Áluinn,* the Four Beautiful Persons. In Synge's play the saint restores the sight of Martin and Mary Doul, an old beggar couple. But with sight, they discover that rather than being handsome and beautiful as they had imagined, they were old and ugly, and they experience some of the nastiness of the sighted world. In time their vision begins to dim again. When the saint returns and offers to effect his cure a second time, they refuse and wander off into their own darkening world.

Isn't it finer sights ourselves had a while since and we sitting dark smelling the sweet beautiful smells do be rising in the warm nights and hearing the swift flying things racing in the air, till we'd be looking up in our own minds into a grand sky, and seeing lakes, and broadening rivers, and hills are waiting for the spade and plough.

The lesson is that it is our own special vision that brings us wonders and glories rather than the material beauty of the world. As old Martin says:

I'm thinking it's a good right ourselves have to be sitting blind, hearing a soft wind turning round the little leaves of the spring and feeling the sun, and we not tormenting our souls with the sight of the grey days, and the holy men, and the dirty feet is trampling the world.

6

The Rituals

They first make on their knees the rounds of certain places three times, and also drink of the Well: they then wade barefoot throughout the stream, through the Theachra or Thurrus, a small lane through which flows a stream from the Holy Well, while praying all the time. This lane, in summer time, is full of thistles, briars and nettles, so much so, that several times a person making the pilgrimage is completely hidden by them, and the place is soft under foot, with numerous sharp stones in the way, none of which may be removed. Next they proceed to each of the ruined chapels (there are four) in succession, and recite certain prayers at each of these stations. They finish each round by praying at the old cross. They then enter the largest of the ruined churches where they pray round an old stone slab there, nine times, saying a Pater and Ave each time, and placing a small stone on the slab after each round: then they go into the inner building and after praying under the east window where the altar once stood, they finish by putting a leaf in the window and kissing the stone under the window inside. They then come out and sitting down on a grave, put their shoes on their feet. They conclude by bestowing an alms on the poor, of whom there are sure to be several present on the feastdays referred to.

So wrote one Canon John O'Hanlon about the year 1870, describing the scene at St Mullin's in County Carlow.

'Rounds' are the most familiar features of holy-well rituals, and these have very often been incorporated into modern Christian devotions, even where Masses are celebrated at the site. The devotee will encircle the well usually three times (or three times three) uttering set prayers or invocations. Always clockwise, sunwise. Anti-sunwise movements are not only considered unlucky but blasphemous also and could bring severe retribution on the person and/or his or her cattle. Very often 'beds' or mounds are associated with the well. These also would be encircled, and the traditional way to count prayers is to take a handful of stones of the correct number, and drop one on the 'bed' with each set of prayers completed. The size of the cairns of pebbles at some sites shows for how long the piles have been added to. Magic circles, magic numbers. If a fish is seen in the well, this is a very auspicious omen.

Wading through the well is a special feature of the rite at St Mullin's. The site is named after St Moling (variously spelt Mullin, Molen or Moh-ling) who, according to the annals, died in AD 697. St Mullin's is a particularly charming spot on the River Barrow. It is framed by a ridge of the Blackstairs mountains, and has a long ecclesiastical history. A stream runs by the monastery site towards the Barrow and this, according to tradition, is a mill-race dug by St Moling. Part of the well is now enclosed by high walls and the pilgrim enters through a doorway and, barefoot of course, wades 'against the stream' which, apparently, is the way it was done by the saint. During the Middle Ages this was a famous pilgrimage. Great cures were claimed, particularly for ulcers. Children's heads used to be held under a spout which channels some of the water into the well house.

17 June was St Moling's Day. The feast of St James, 25 July, was also celebrated and, like several other Pattern Days, it was a great day for the surrounding district, featuring various celebrations, dances and contests.

I joined the Pattern Day in 1998. The Bicentenary of the Rising of 1798, which had such momentous consequences in this part of Carlow/Wexford, was being celebrated at the same time, and both events were amalgamated. There was the spectacle of an army of men (and some women also) in green jackets armed with pikes marching on the monastery site. Attendant maidens in long dresses and ruffled headgear sheltered among the ruins as the rain came down

relentlessly. Sentinels on the hill stood heroically in the torrents for hours on end as Mass was concelebrated on an altar contrived from one of the tombs under a dripping garland. It was, in fact, very moving, and it was a pity that the weather caused the curtailment of some of the entertainments which had been planned for later. The rain didn't deter many of those attending the Mass and other prayers from making their way, already drenched, to the well to pay their respects and perform some of the rituals.

The same saint is honoured at Mullinakill in County Kilkenny, which claims to be his birthplace. Legend says he left Mullinakill after a row with a local lady. Moling, it seems, had leg ulcers (so his wells have a cure for that affliction) and the lady's cows used to lick them to ease them. However, for some reason, instead of increasing their flow of milk, the cows' good deed caused the milk 'to go back', in other words to decrease in flow. So their owner cursed the saint and he, disgruntled, went off to found his subsequently famous monastery by the Barrow.

At Castlekeeran, a young tree replaces the 'hoary ash tree of surpassing size and beauty' described in 1849.

Opposite page: St Moling's Well, County Carlow. In 1998 the 1798 commemoration ceremonies were combined with the Pattern on a very wet day.

Pattern Day at Castlekeeran.

At Mullinakill, St Moling's Well is at the bottom of a steep slope below a narrow road. Steps lead down past a modern statue and a modern 'altar' has been built on the lower part for latter-day rituals. Looking down the slope from the road, the dominating feature is a large ancient skeleton of a tree through which a thorn tree is now growing. The custom of taking twigs to protect the home from fire for the coming year has taken a heavy toll on the old tree and it remains to be seen whether the power will be transferred to the thorn tree when it can no longer bear the burden. Beyond the tree, higher up the slope, a pure spring emerges from the hillside whence it is caught and piped into a stone-lined trough, making it easy to reach. The streamlet then trickles around the tree clockwise before disappearing into the ground.

An old stone-built altar under the shelter of the tree has a small 'tabernacle' and numerous trinkets, statues and rosaries are left here. It also bears a pile of stones, which is added to by each pilgrim. In addition, a series of white-painted metal crosses around the slope mark the 'stations'.

I was lucky enough to attend a Pattern Day there on a gorgeous sunny day. Even before I arrived I could see that there was a celebratory atmosphere in the air. Groups of people and many cars were heading in the same direction. Cars were parked on the verges of the already very narrow road but the inconvenience didn't seem to bother anyone, leading instead to cheerful and good-natured banter. Near the site, stalls were set up, selling sweets and soft drinks and offering prizes for loops or darts. Some people had brought along stools and deck-chairs and settled themselves on the road verge overlooking the site. All in all there was a great feeling of a holiday. The chief celebrant of Mass arrived, attended by four other priests, and a grand sight it was, the priests' white robes, which fluttered a little in the light breeze, standing out against the green of the grass and the rising hillside beyond, in the bright sunshine after a shower.

St Lassair's Well at Kilronan, County Roscommon, is one of my favourites. First of all because of its idyllic situation, beside the rush-fringed water at the eastern end of Lough Meelagh, close to the ruins of the church where Turlough O'Carolan, last of the Gaelic bards, is buried. The well site is well cared for and has been tamed and landscaped since I first visited it many years ago, but not excessively. A metal cross on a seven-foot plinth erected during the Holy Year of 1975 bears a plaque outlining the quite lengthy ritual devotions of the 'Station'. These include the usual rounds of prayers, at the cross, at a modern statue of Our Lady, at the well and plaque, and at the 'altar', with further prayers at the nearby cemetery. 'Touch the water with finger-tips and make the Sign of the Cross.' The well is enclosed by a stone wall with three steps leading down to the beautifully clear waters. There are votive offerings there, little statues of the Virgin, rosaries, medals, pens and other small personal items. The water runs through an opening to a further stone-lined passage, this also reached by steps ending in a hollow stone known as the Holy Font, which appears to be a bullaun (old grinding) stone. It continues under stone slabs through the undergrowth until it is lost in the rushes which edge the lake. Washing of the feet, hands and face in the 'holy font' were part of the older ritual. The plaque does not include the healing ritual for those with backache (a common ailment in times of hard agricultural labour) of crawling under the 'altar' while invoking the older or newer gods, according to disposition. I make a point of carrying out this ritual any time I call by and so far, thank God, my back is in reasonable shape. On the other hand, with a bad back it would be a difficult feat to accomplish.

I have never succeeded in catching a Pattern or any rituals in progress, despite being there a few times on the traditional day, 15 August. It seems that formal Christianised devotions — Mass and prayers — have been moved to some Sundays in August and September. I gather that devotions are held on more than one Sunday. There is another old well across the road on the hill to the left of the graveyard. Though not 'holy' in the traditional sense, in the past emigrants used to bring away some clay from close to the well to keep them safe from illness.

Another well with obviously ancient healing rituals, besides being quite a beautiful place ('one of the most beautiful holy wells in Ireland' according to Sir William Wilde) is St Ciarán's Well at Castlekeeran

The 'altar' at St Lassair's Well at Kilronan, County Roscommon.

near Kells in County Meath. In Wilde's day it was 'shaded by a hoary ash tree of surpassing size and beauty'. That tree has disappeared but a younger tree stands in its place. It bears its burden of ribbons and rags gaily. The well is close to the road, in a slight hollow. The spring, emerging from a small hillock, rises and sinks three times to make three small rock-enclosed channels. Each channel has its distinct cure, one for sore feet (surely one greatly needed by so many otherwise healthy people), one for headache and toothache, one for backache. There is also a place allocated for drinking, and that is equipped with a ladle. Little plaques inform visitors of the correct rites. Backache sufferers seat themselves in an appropriately shaped seat in the rock; others dabble their bare feet in the water to keep them free from soreness during the coming year. It has been shown that the water is very pure and rich in calcium carbonate. I was lucky enough to attend a Pattern here on the first Sunday of August (a Lughnasa festival) in 1998. A crowd of well over a hundred had

gathered and there was a great holiday atmosphere. Young and old alike were doing the 'rounds' and immersions. That year Meath was playing in the football Provincial Final and many sported the green Meath football jerseys, giving quite a unique flavour to the devotions. In accordance with custom, I dabbled my feet in the appropriate channel and, on a hot August day, found the water to be icy cold. One old man seated on the rock beside me, whose feet I admired for their strong youthful look, told me he came every year of his life.

It is all a wonderful amalgam of ancient and Christian rites. There is a small oratory where it is lovely to attend, sitting or kneeling on the grass, as the Mass is celebrated by the local Parish Priest. A festive day follows with a band playing, tug-of-war contests and other sports, ending with a lively night's fun.

Much folklore surrounds St Ciarán's Well. For instance, the healing powers depend on the correct day, and are at their most potent at midnight before the Pattern, gradually subsiding over the next twenty-four hours. The very lucky may even see the sacred trout which can make its appearance shortly after midnight. This is a sure sign of favour. Well into the twentieth century, horses used to be driven through the water at midnight to keep them safe through the year ahead. These are very ancient concepts, surviving wonderfully here and in some other places. The great Bronze Age cemeteries of Loughcrew look down over this plain, and it comes to my mind that the people who built them may well have worshipped at the spring which is now St Ciarán's Well.

There is an old graveyard nearby which is associated with the remnants of a monastery founded by Ciarán. In it stand three high crosses, somewhat plain in design. The base of a fourth one is known to be in the river nearby though I confess I could not see it in the brown waters. Inevitably, there is a story about how it got there. At nearby Kells there was an important foundation of St Colmcille's, some remnants of which are still to be seen (and which are worth visiting, especially for the four very fine high crosses in the grounds of the Protestant Parish Church). Not unusually there was rivalry between the two establishments. It seems that when Colmcille saw the crosses at Ciarán's monastery, he coveted them, removed three of them to Kells at night, and was caught in the act with the fourth one. When challenged, in a typical fit of Colmcillian temper he threw it in the river. As those at Kells are much finer than those at Castlekeeran, and of a later date, he must have been persuaded to return the three he made off with but subsequently established his superiority by commissioning even better and bigger ones for his own monastery.

The Rag-tree, Boherard

They might have come on the wind,

these rags and tatters, or drifted down

the current of the ditch to dangle there

like seaweed. They were the bright hand-me-down

foliage of that thorn tree in winter.

Poor sinners came, warts and all,

For the holy water of that holy well.

They left loose tokens of a patchwork shawl,

Prayed, and promised to return.

They say it stood since God was a boy,

a twisted stick of offerings

no weather could destroy.

It fell in our time. This was told to me

by one of a lost community

at the crossroads of Knocklough,

that lived from hand to mouth, past pity,

and held the rest of the world

long in the gaze of its one eye.

It will pass like their names,

Snows, Laws, *into the legends of incubi.*

Well they might have hung their coat

on that hawthorn bush at Boherard

or come to kneel near the church

where, late one night, at the graveyard

gate, a big tree moved. We heard it stood

three hundred years, heard tell of the way

it simply took up roots and walked.

Anyway it moved. Or so they say.

Peter Fallon

Opposite page: Rag Tree and Wart Stone at Dysartgallen, County Laois. Testimonials to the efficacy of the site have come in sworn statements from as far away as the state of Oregon.

7

'The Saint's Road'

The Irish word for well is Tobar. The Irish Townlands Index lists no fewer than 163 place names beginning with Tobar, Tobber or Tubbrid. I know no way of counting the number that finish with it or incorporate the word in another position.

Ballintubber Abbey in County Mayo is another example of an important ecclesiastical establishment developing from what must have originally been a place of pre-Christian worship. Ballintubber is 'The Townland of the Well' and the well must have been a feature of importance from remote times. It acquired the name of St Patrick's Well when that saint established a church there around the year 440. An Abbey was founded on the site by Cathal Crovdearg O'Connor, King of Connacht, in 1216. It has since become known as 'The Abbey that refused to die' and its story is certainly unique. For almost 800 years Mass has been offered every Sunday within its walls despite suffering fire, suppression and proscription. During all the wars and persecutions it was never abandoned. A photograph taken in 1865 shows a congregation kneeling on the grass-covered ground of the roofless church. Mainly through the relentless efforts of one modest and mild-mannered man, the Rev Thomas Egan, full restoration of the Abbey began in the 1960s and today it is an important centre for pilgrimage and retreat, visited by thousands every year.

The well would have been a cult well, thus inviting a Christianising intervention — in this case supplied, according to tradition, by St Patrick. And the well now? Somewhat unfortunately, it stands in the middle of a golf course some 500 yards outside the Abbey walls, but is accessible to anyone who is willing to risk ducking their heads when they hear the shout of 'Fore'. It has been 'done up' in recent years — no doubt to protect it from rough golfers — and now bears the legend 'Tobar le Padraic, 441 AD', with a verse from St Patrick's Breastplate, that lovely invocation which itself seems to echo the imagined sound of ancient incantations:

Christ be with me, Christ within me,
Christ behind me, Christ before me,
Christ beside me, Christ to win me
Christ to comfort and restore me
Christ beneath me, Christ above me...

'Tobar le Pádraig' St Patrick's Well, outside the walls of Ballintubber Abbey, County Mayo. The Abbey has been beautifully restored and is an important centre for pilgrimage and retreat.

Croagh Patrick, Ireland's holy mountain. An ancient pilgrimage trackway leading from Ballintubber Abbey to the mountain has been restored. It is about 35 kilométres long and, among other features, has five holy wells along its route.

Courtesy Bord Fáilte

An early pilgrimage road led from Ballintubber Abbey to the summit of Croagh Patrick, Ireland's holy mountain. In honour of the Jubilee Year 2000, which the Church designated The Year of the Pilgrimage, funds were made available for the refurbishment of a number of similar pilgrimage routes such as The Saint's Road on the Dingle Peninsula and St Kevin's Road at Glendalough. The Croagh Patrick road from Ballintubber had already been largely renewed by local voluntary effort, with marked signposts and stiles along the way. Here and there some flags from the original paved pathway were uncovered. It is the longest of those surviving, its length being reckoned at about thirty-five kilometres (twenty-two miles) 'as the crow flies' ('a demented crow', someone remarked). It takes about eleven hours to negotiate the full route, with attendant rituals, to the base of the Reek — that is, of course, before starting up the mountain. A booklet sets the route out step by step.

The singular outline of Croagh Patrick would have made it a revered mountain from earliest times and the path may originally have led all the way from Cruachan, a huge complex of earthworks which was known as the royal residence of the Kings of Connacht. Apart from the wells and various ecclesiastical features along the way, there is a large rock at Bohey which is inscribed with circles and cup-marks of a style associated with the Bronze Age, symbols possibly related to sun-worship.

There are no fewer than five wells designated as holy wells along the route. First, 'Tobar na Cannuana' or the Well of the Canons, where Easter ceremonies took place in Early Christian times. It is reputed to have a cure for blindness. Like many, but not all wells, it is stipulated that the water could not be used for profane purposes such as feeding of cattle or washing of clothes. Next comes the Well of the Stringle, re-christened Cranereen Well, where St Patrick is recorded as having spent 'over two Sundays' baptising and teaching. Aghagower has a round tower, 'Dabhach Phádraig', a kind of circular bath, and The Well of the Deacons which now appears to have dried up. St Brendan's Well at Lankill is particularly interesting. It contains an oval stone which sufferers apply to their ailing parts in hope of a cure. How it came to be associated with St Brendan is not recorded. The great antiquity of use of the well for cult purposes is suggested by a number of bronze age items in the immediate locality, including a nine-foot pillar stone with concentric circles engraved on it and a cist burial chamber. The next well, at Bohey, is close to the decorated rock mentioned above.

I have wondered whether Ogulla Well near Tulsk was originally associated with Cruachan, as it is so close to the site. The well, on the Ballintober (not to be confused with Ballintubber above) Road, is one which has acquired a large following, attracting hundreds of pilgrims every year. The name comes from Oigh-Ghiolla, a sixth century saint, and stories of miracle cures are abundant. According to tradition, St Patrick baptised Etna and Fidelma, the daughters of the high king, at this site.

The site is a large and elaborately landscaped one. The spring gushes out in a strong stream from the rocky bank and flows onward in a widening brook. A modern six-sided glass-faced chapel rises above it: inside on the altar there are offerings and hand-written petitions. A set of Stations of the Cross has been marked out among the surrounding greenery. There is a statue of St Patrick, and a small statue of the Blessed Virgin. An ash tree covered with rags over-hangs the stream, and offerings of medals, pictures, flowers and other objects show that the old cult still lives side by side with the celebration of Mass, sometimes by the local bishop, on the last Sunday of June. Stone walls and a bench make for a most soothing and restful place. In the summer of 1997 the *Roscommon Champion* reported a number of 'miracle cures' including that of a man with a lump over one eye who had been told it would have to be surgically removed; many stories are told of cures by sufferers from cancer, arthritis, eyesores and aching limbs.

Not far from Ogulla, at Toberaraght, off the Ballaghaderreen road, is St Attracta's Well, which gives the name to the townland. Tradition claims that the saint took the veil from St Patrick himself here. According to the Book of Armagh, it was here that the shape of the Celtic Cross miraculously came into being, to provide a paten for St Patrick in his celebration of the Mass. The spring is in a fairly deep cavity surrounded by a semi-circular wall, obviously renovated in recent times. It incorporates a small stone roughly shaped like a cross. Four steep steps lead down to the well from a narrow stile in the wall. The water flows into a second well-shaped enclosure and along a channel to cross under the road and become a stream around an old estate wall. The day I visited, a bunch of flowers had been left there, though it was neither August nor September, when Mass and/or rosary are sometimes said.

Ogulla Well (Tobar Oigh-Ghoilla) near Tulsk. Devotions are held regularly in the chapel (on left of picture) and there are many accounts of cures.

8

Discoveries and Surprises

hen there are the surprise discoveries. Some of these wanderings into what I might call deepest Ireland have been rewarded with quite unexpected treasures. As part of the Jubilee Year 2000 church celebrations, parishes all over Ireland were adopting different ways of marking the year. In the diocese of Ossory, Saighir Ciaráin or Seir Kieran six miles (eight kilometres) south east of Birr, near Clareen) has always been an important place. A monastery was established by St Ciarán the Elder in very early Christian times (he was a contemporary of St Patrick) on what was already probably a pagan sanctuary, where according to legend a perpetual fire was kept alight, as it was in Brigid's Kildare. The well is some hundreds of yards from the site of the monastery. Contained now in a concrete basin about eight foot square, it could hardly be called beautiful, but it is obviously regarded with great respect. A car park has been laid out next to it, indicating its contemporary popularity. The water runs pure and clear. On 5 March 2000, the parish organised a pilgrimage to its holy places on this, the traditional Pattern day, and included not only the well and the monastic remains, but the well-known St Ciarán's Bush.

Trees, as we have seen, often play an important part in holy well rituals. Special trees were sacred to the Celts. The oldest Gaelic alphabet is based on associations with trees. It was known as the Beth-Luis-Nion, which are the first three letters, each of which is a tree — Birch, Rowan, Ash. Druidic colleges were founded in wood groves. In folklore, some trees are regarded as immortal, some won't burn, dire consequences would follow anyone who dared to cut down or even damage a special tree. Oak, holly, hazel and whitethorn were the most sacred.

St Ciarán's Bush, really a well-decorated Rag Tree, is a successor to an ancient tree of which only the stump now remains. It has stood in the centre of the road for decades. Originally it stood on the side of the road. In time, as traffic increased, it was necessary to widen the road. The tree, however, by local sentiment, could not be touched. The Local Authority assented and the road was re-planned to leave the tree standing in a little green oasis in the centre. In more recent times, heavier traffic demanded further road widening. A compromise has been reached and, though the roadway on one side is now wider than the other and takes the bulk of motorised traffic, the 'Bush' still maintains its position. It was pleasing to see the modern Pilgrimage, led by the parish priest, accord the same respect to it and to the well as it did to the monastic site and the local parish church.

I had gone that day especially for the Saighir Ciaráin Pattern. As I was in the area, I decided to make a call to Lemonaghan (Liath Manchain, the seat of St Manchan) a few miles north of Ferbane, County Offaly where, it was said, right into modern times, milk could never be sold, only given, because of a story relating to Manchan and a cow. The well here, like that at Saighir Ciaráin, is obviously in constant use and is well cared for. It is enclosed by a keyhole-shaped wall, with steps leading down to the water. Here also the water appears clear and pure, and good to drink. It also has its blessed tree — a miraculous ash indeed, as it is so hollowed out and damaged one wonders how it manages to cling to life. Rags and rosaries, strings, ribbons and medals hang on it. To it, it was recorded in 1886, 'the blind, lame and persons afflicted with other chronic diseases, come on the anniversary of the patron saint's death' (24 January). A little garden of meditation has been contrived from the corner of a field adjoining the well and an air of peace and tranquillity reigns there. In the graveyard adjoining some ruined structures, a plaque reads:

Liath Manchain Church stands on site of monastery founded by St Manchan before his death in the plague of 664. There are old grave slabs, maybe ninth/tenth century. Church dates partly from twelfth, partly fifteenth century. To the east, a stone building called 'the cell of St Manchan's mother.' The fine twelfth century shrine of St Manchan preserved not far away in parish church at Boher.

I was somewhat puzzled. Had I not seen St Manchan's Shrine in the National Museum in Dublin? I found Boher with a little difficulty: a smallish church where there was no village, just a few scattered houses, no pub or shops. After all, what could be more anonymous than 'Boher' meaning merely a road? Could this really be the place? A sign outside said yes, and here, astonishingly, is one of the treasures of the nation, the largest and probably most ancient reliquary in Ireland.

The shrine is a gabled box of yew wood shaped like an early church, about sixty-two cm long and forty-eight cm high (over two foot long and nineteen inches high). It is decorated all over with gilt, bronze and enamelled fittings in an elaborately interlaced style and eleven of the original fifty bronze figures which once ornamented it still remain.

St Manchan's Shrine. This photograph is of a facsimile, held in the National Museum in Dublin; the original reliquary is located in Boher Church in County Offaly. *Photo: National Museum of Ireland*

An entry in the Annals of the Four Masters for the year 1166 states: 'The shrine of Manchan, of Maethail, was covered by Ruaidhrí Ua Conchobhair, and an embroidery of gold was carried over it by him, in as good a style as a relic was ever covered in Ireland.' If this is the shrine in question, and if there were originally gold fittings, these have disappeared, and the bronze figures are of a later date. The bones inside are presumed to be the bones of the saint and I was told locally that some of the bones have signs of arteriosclerosis, so the saint has a special cure for arthritis.

The shrine left the district on only a few very brief occasions: in 1853 and 1882 for the Dublin Exhibitions, and in 1935 and 1970 for maintenance at the British Museum. Guardians of the reliquary were the Buckleys, who claimed inherited rights from the last recorded abbot of Lemonaghan. When the medieval church fell to ruin in the eighteenth century the shrine was removed to a thatched barn church at Cooldorrough. It was moved to its present church in 1860.

A facsimile was made at one stage which was what I had seen in the Museum.

That a small, relatively obscure community has managed to maintain the precious relic of its patron saint and its shrine through eight hundred often turbulent years is quite a remarkable phenomenon.

The church at Boher has other treasures too. Behind the shrine rises a magnificent stained glass window showing the saint and the shrine. It is one of five windows in this small church from the famous Harry Clarke Studios, windows which were completed just before the great artist died in 1931 at the age of forty-one.

There is a poem ascribed to the same Manchan, one of those lovely nature poems so full of sweetness that were characteristic of the early monks in Ireland. Its opening verses, as translated by Frank O'Connor:

Grant me sweet Christ the grace to find —
Son of the living God! —
A small hut in a lonesome spot
To make it my abode.

A little pool but very clear
To stand beside the place
Where all men's sins are washed away
By sanctifying grace...

Over a thousand years later people still come to 'the little pool' to have their troubles washed away.

St Ciarán's Bush stands on an island in the middle of the road. Local sentiment would not allow it to be disturbed when the road was being widened.

9

Fore and its Seven Wonders

In the old annals St Feichin is described as 'A Man, abstinent, pleasant, charitable, powerful, slender-bellied, just-worded, honest, pious, rich in sense, godly, affectionate, discreet, opportune, wise, prayerful, skilful, righteous, holy-worded, active(?), chaste, possessed of illuminated books, to wit, a man of a bright, summery life, an abbot and an anchorite, fair-worded Feichin of Fore, from the delightful borders of Luigne, from the loveable province of Connaught.'

When he died a huge column in the likeness of the colours of the rainbow was seen stretching from his monastery up to heaven. After his death, Satan was asked whether he had come to try to disturb the soul of Feichin as he lay dying. Satan answered 'Not only were we unable to do ought to him, but until the end of seven days after his death we durst not visit Ireland because of the splendour of the Holy Ghost which surrounded it.'

St Feichin's Well with Fore Abbey in the background. The ash tree growing from the well suffers from the unusual custom of coins being imbedded in its bark. The 'water [of the well] which will not boil' is one of the seven wonders of Fore.

A fine eulogy, to be sure. The bearer of such powerful virtue was born in County Sligo around 580 AD. Feichin's monastery at Fore in County Westmeath was the largest and most important of the several that he founded. At the height of its renown it housed no fewer than 300 monks.

Fore is located close to Castlepollard and its name in Irish, Fobhar Feichin, means Feichin's Spring. Feichin founded monasteries also on Omey Island, County Galway (q.v.), at High Island off the Galway coast, at Cong between Loughs Corrib and Mask and at Termonfeckin, County Louth.

Sick children were immersed in St Feichin's Bath, a stone-lined vat near the well.

Fore today, apart from being a very pretty, if tiny, village, is rather an amazing place, with remains not only of Feichin's Church (or, rather, one of its successors, as the original wooden church was burned repeatedly over the centuries) but also of an imposing thirteenth century Benedictine Priory, a charming columbarium or dove-cot, two towers, two gateways, a fifteenth century anchorite's cell and the remnants of a mill. There is also, of course, the holy well.

Fore is famous for its 'Seven Wonders'. These, according to local tradition, consist of:

1. *Water which will not boil.* This refers to the water of St Feichin's Well. Even *attempting* to boil it will bring ill luck.

2. *Wood which will not burn.* The old ash tree which traditionally had three branches in honour of the trinity has now, alas, only one. It may have resisted fire, but it didn't manage to resist the damage resulting from the practice of hammering coins into the trunk.

3. *Water which flows uphill.* The water which turned St Feichin's Mill, which was in use until the late 1800s and replaced by another which was in use until about 1950, appeared to flow uphill from nearby Lough Lene.

4. *The Abbey in a quaking bog.* It is true that the land on which the abbey stands is bogland. However, it has been shown that the building stands on a firm spot, well chosen, and drainage has firmed up the surrounding area.

5. *A mill without a race.* See 3 above. When St Feichin had the mill built, the millwright complained that there was no water to turn it. So Feichin went to Lough Lene, struck the ground and the water 'flowed uphill' to the mill.

6. *The Anchorite in a Stone.* This 'wonder' is factual. The small intact building on the opposite side of the road incorporates a genuine anchorite's cell, the last occupant of which was one

Patrick Begley in the mid-1600s. Fore and its lands had been granted in 1588 to the Nugents, Baronets of Delvin, one of whom restored the cell and incorporated it into a mausoleum for his own family.

7. *Stone raised by St Feichin's prayers.* It is clear to many that the huge trabeate lintel stone above the doorway of St Feichin's church could only have been raised by supernatural means.

St Feichin's Church, which stands in the sloping cemetery above the road, is the oldest building on the site, portions of it dating, it has been estimated, from the tenth century. It was part of the earlier monastery that stood here in the thirteenth century before the arrival of the Benedictines. The stone lintel over the doorway which, we are told, was raised with the intervention of the saint is typical of early Irish churches, though this is an unusually massive one.

The well is situated close to the modern car park and is often visited, though the traditional Pattern days of St Feichin's Day, 20 January and St John's Day, 24 June, do not appear to be particularly honoured. Its water is regarded as being especially useful for toothache and headache. A tree grows out of the well, its one remaining limb struggling valiantly to survive the unusual custom, already mentioned, of hammering coins into the wood. It has a crowning of rags as well as coins. There is a stone-lined 'bath' a short distance away in which sick children used to be immersed. It has an ash tree beside it, and it too is festooned with rags and coins.

There are a number of stone crosses, fourteen at least, scattered around the adjoining townlands, and also various earthworks which have not, as yet, been excavated. There is so much to Fore and its surroundings that it is surprising that it has not been more 'developed' and landscaped. However, much of its special charm arises from the fact that it has not been commercialised and that it remains in a state of natural simplicity.

10

... Toberara's Well Flows

How oft have I drank of Toberara's well

They say in its water there is a great spell

Where the sick and afflicted can cure all

their woe

And it's into the Barrow Toberara's well

flows.

Toberara, or Tubberara. Some say it means the well of St Bara, others the well by the Barrow. Others again speculate that it means 'The Well of the Slaughter', as there are accounts in the annals of a great battle fought near here in 475 AD, possibly arising out of tributes being exacted on the local chieftain by the king of Leinster. The present bridge over the young Barrow indicates that there was once a ford here, always a place to be defended. The fallen warriors would have given rise to a grave-yard, and it is true that during local building and drainage works many skeletons were found. It would have been consecrated when a Christian church was established, but no sign of the church remains.

But I anticipate. What took me to Toberara on a fine morning in May 2000 was a news item in *The Nationalist* (of Kildare) that:

Athy pilgrims will walk to Toberara Well on Sunday, 21 May.

It is an example of many wells which had fallen into disuse but were revitalised during, and in honour of, the Millennium Jubilee Year, when it was hoped 'that people will rediscover early pilgrimage routes and Christian settlements in their own area'.

The pilgrimage was to begin at the town of Athy. Pilgrims would make the three-kilometre (two-mile) pilgrimage on foot (although the traditional bare feet were not demanded), stopping occasionally for 'stations' *en route*. Unfortunately I couldn't get there on 21 May, but decided to visit the site on the following day. The Athy Heritage Centre directed me to the premises of Frank O'Brien, merchant and publican in the Square. I presented myself to Frank, a most

charming and gracious, erect and youthful-looking man in his eighties. Between himself and a few of his early morning customers, I soon had more wells listed than I could visit in a lifetime. He did persuade me, however, that whatever wells I chose to ignore, I just had to visit St Patrick's Well at Glasealy. We'll come to that later.

As instructed, I called to Mrs Hickey at Bert Crossroads, which is on the Monasterevin Road from Athy, and her son guided me most of the way from there. Toberara is found by turning right at the crossroads, then, at a bridge over the Barrow, turning left into a field, and swinging to the right. The old graveyard is located in the far corner. Even with directions it was hard enough to locate, and I must confess I did a fair bit of walking through several fields before I found the place (the tramping of hundreds of feet the day before had left no impression that I could see). The tops of a few cypress trees seen over the old hedgerow provide a clue. Mrs Hickey told me that the well was

Toberara's Well, in spite of the song, does not flow very well now, but devotion to it has been rekindled since the Jubilee Year 2000.

St Patrick's Well, Glasealy, County Kildare.

dedicated to St John the Baptist and that patterns had taken place traditionally on St John's Day, 24 June, but had been discontinued a long time ago. This year's pilgrimage was a very welcome revival.

The graveyard is tiny, with only a handful of grave sites — local names such as Brennans, Rowans (also spelt Ruen on the same headstone), Hickeys, Barrys, Fitzpatricks, Chandlers and Kavanaghs. It had obviously been very overgrown before it was cleared for this special occasion. The last funeral there was in 1985. The 'well' at this stage didn't look much like a well, but rather a scoop in the ground filled with water, at the bottom of which could be seen the stones that once presumably surrounded and protected it. An old ash tree leans over it but in this instance there is no sign of rags or pins. The well has been affected by drainage work on the Barrow and when it holds water at all (which, miraculously one might say, it did on the sunny day of the jubilee pilgrimage) the water is crystal clear. I was told that the pilgrimage day had been a great occasion, finishing with the Toberara ballad sung beautifully by a local singer, after prayers and hymns. People sat around on the grass in the sunshine, greeted friends and chatted to neighbours — a real community gathering. Surely after such a day the well and cemetery will be maintained by a new generation.

I am indebted to Frank O'Brien for the lyrics of the ballad. Also, by courtesy of a tape sent on by Frank, I have heard it sung sweetly by Mary Prior, whose grandparents lived at Toberara long ago.

Toberara

How oft have I stood on the Bridge of Athy
And gazed on those waters, that flow
gently by.
Oh! How sweetly, how neatly, how gently
they go
And it's into the Barrow Toberara's well
flows.

How oft have I drank of Toberara's well
They say in its water there is a great spell
Where the sick and afflicted can cure all
their woe
And it's into the Barrow Toberara's well
flows.

How oft have I swam in the Barrow
sweet tide
And walked with my thoughts down by
Lord's Island side
And gazed at the waters so easy and slow
And it's into the Barrow Toberara's well
flows.

So here's to my Home and my exquisite
joy
Once again will I stand on the Bridge of
Athy
And gaze at those waters so gentle below
And it's into the Barrow Toberara's well
flows.

For my heart's in old Ireland across the
blue wave
My heart's in old Ireland the home of the
brave
'Tis the home of the brave where the
wild shamrocks grow
And it's into the Barrow Toberara's well
flows.

We know that these wells were honoured through long centuries. They did not, therefore, arrange themselves conveniently for modern motor traffic, even though our modern roads often follow old trackways. So usually, when looking for a well, local guidance is needed. I have many recollections of wading waist-deep through wild-flower meadows and bracken or over rocks in an attempt to locate wells clearly marked on the map — sometimes even with the help of a local person. Toberara had taken some finding. So too did Glasealy, though I had directions from three people — maybe that was the trouble.

The Local History Guide explained that St Patrick's Well at Glasealy is a very active shrine, much visited at any time, with a big pilgrimage on St Patrick's Day. For a stranger though, it is hard to find. Coming from Athy on the Dublin Road, one turns right at Fontstown Cross, and then takes the second next right turn. After a graveyard (itself worth exploring) and opposite the second gateway to a large house, there's a field gateway with a stile. If you advance up the hill across the field, you should be able to discern the well enclosure down to the left among the trees.

To tell the truth, I didn't mind my pointless searchings on that day. This is remote and deeply rural countryside, with small wandering roads, old flowery hedgerows, trees arching overhead filtering the brightness. In the slumberous afternoon sun there was only the sound of the occasional distant tractor and the lowing of cows; even the birds seemed quiet as if was too much bother to sing. My own motor incursion seemed an unmannerly intrusion.

Legend says that St Patrick, while travelling in this area, was warned by Briga, a Christian of the Hy Barrche tribe, of snares and ambushes set for him by his enemies. Some of the local chieftains were converted to Christianity and asked St Patrick to bless the nearby well as was the custom. Like most of these holy wells, the water is said to have curative properties.

A tastefully landscaped setting now surrounds the well. There are lawns and flowers and trees. A small stream is captured which flows under and around some natural rock terraces which are a feature of the garden surround. The stream divides, moving among the lawns and joins again to 'bicker down the valley'. A third streamlet emerges from under the rocks to join the divided stream to create a miniature gathering of waters. Under an old ash tree and intertwined whitethorn, the well is sunk in a rock basin which is partly natural and partly man-made. The whitethorn bears a few rags and tokens. Cups hang on a branch for the use of visitors.

Some may find it over-landscaped but I found it a serene and contemplative place, touching in the devotion lavished on its upkeep by a purely voluntary group. A nice stylised statue (by Dick Joynt) of St Patrick carrying a bird and staff overlooks it all. Its ordered calm was unexpected among the wide meadows.

As one of the locals remarked, this area is 'thick with holy wells'. Within a short distance, there is Belan near Moone, Kellistown (where misfortune followed a cottier who dared to cut down one of the sacred trees), Rathvilly (site of the baptism in 450 of Crimthann, King of Leinster, who was a persecutor of Christians up till then), Graney (where a wicked landlord who tried to fill in the well grew a tail). All of these are St Patrick's Wells. A well near Drumlane monastery is dedicated to St Mogue, as is another at Kilnacross in Kildallan parish. The same saint established a church at Rossinver by Lough Melvin's shore, where he died and was buried. His well near the lakeshore is a fine crystal clear spring. Others in the Diocese of Kilmore alone are St Brigid's at Ballinamore, St Dympna's at Lower Lavey, St Patrick's at Shancor, Kilmainhamwood.... I could go on.

Then there was the day that four of us searched high up and low down in a small valley near Renvyle in Connemara for the Well of the Seven Daughters, which we knew to be the well associated with, and therefore close to, the ruined Church of the same name, and which one of the party remembered having seen several years back. Who these Seven Daughters, or Sisters, were, nobody seems to know but their cult was widespread in Connemara. The historian Roderick O'Flaherty, writing of West Connacht, identified six churches named for them, including one on the island

A cross-marked stone is the only clue to the *Well of the Seven Daughters,* near Renvyle, in Connemara.

of Inisheer. O'Flaherty refers to them as Daughters of the King of Britain, but that sounds like a local guess of the time. The magical number seven may indicate an older association.

But to our search. Even a local man joined in without success. When we were about to give up, we noticed, on a flat stone near our feet, the faintly discernible mark of a cross. A clue! We searched around it, but still no well. Then someone suggested lifting the stone and there, under the stone, was our Blessed Well, a small pothole in the turfy ground, at the bottom of which we could see a glint of the sky reflected in moving water. Presumably it had been covered over to prevent an animal breaking a leg, had then become overgrown, and possibly somewhat disrupted because of small drainage works. Pulling at the surrounding sods, we began to uncover portions of a stone structure. In the clay which came away, we found a modern penny coin embedded. Somebody had had recourse to the well in recent years.

It was in 1684 that Roderick O'Flaherty wrote about this as a holy well which was associated with the nearby Church. Even at that stage, the Church itself was already a ruin. Between our small hole in the ground and that once-flourishing establishment, there has been an unbroken connection for over three centuries, and we don't know for how many centuries before that.

Further south in Connemara, at Aillebrack near Ballyconneely, a diligent searcher may uncover, from under its cloak of meadow-sweet and purple loosestrife, another well associated with these Seven Sisters, though there is no evidence here of a church site.

11

Colmcille and Doon

It is 9 June, the feast of the great missioner of Iona, Colmcille (or Colomba, the Latin name by which he is also known). We are in the valley named for him, Glencolmcille, an Irish-speaking glen in the remote southwestern corner of Donegal.

The Atlantic lies ahead, all around rear rugged hills. Along the valley floor lies a collection of monuments covering a period of some 5,000 years, from the megalithic tomb of remote ancestors and decorated pillar-stones of uncertain age, to the monastic remains of Early Christian and medieval foundations, to the relatively 'modern' nineteenth-century Protestant church. Thirteen of these items are the 'stations' of the turas, or Journey, as the pilgrimage is known here.

On this damp morning, bands of pilgrims, some from the valley and nearby, some from far away and overseas, are lined along the five-kilometre (three-and-a-half mile) route, which encircles the valley floor. Most are barefoot, and the route lies over *hard and sometimes stony roadway and across muddy fields edged with nettles and thorns. The turas is a very arduous pilgrimage, perhaps second only to the ascent of Croagh Patrick. It is said that it can be accomplished in three hours, but four hours or longer is not unusual.*

The pilgrim circles each of the thirteen stations sunwise three times, reciting the prescribed prayers — a set number, usually three Our Fathers, Hail Marys and Glorias (spoken in Irish by most of the pilgrims, because this is a Gaeltacht, or Irish-speaking area). There are some archaic practices at a number of the stations. For instance, at the third station, where the pilgrim kneels at the 'place of the knees', he or she then picks up a rounded stone and passes it around his or her body three times. There is a flagstone, St Colmcille's Bed, on which the pilgrim prostrates himself and turns over three times; earth is taken from under a certain stone and carried away. At another, a flat stone is raised to the chin. Colmcille's Well is the seventh station. It is fairly high on the hillside and surrounded by a very large semicircular cairn of stones. Each of the pilgrims has carried three stones up the hill to it. Encircling the cairn and well three times saying the prescribed prayers, for each round they add a stone to the accumulation of centuries. Most of the stones which make up the cairn are a good size, many of them up to a foot across. If they all represent stones carried by pilgrims, they indicate hard work indeed. Then stooping to the well, the pilgrim throws out three drops of water in the name of the Trinity, then drinks of the well water. Nobody is deterred by the inevitable sediment in the normally crystal-clear well caused by the repeated dipping and stirring.

Early Irish hagiology is dominated by the towering figure of Colmcille. He came from the ruling family of the Cenel Conail and was a powerful political and diplomatic figure. He was born in 521 close to Gartan, where a small but very charming Heritage Centre devoted to his life and times stands sheltered by trees by the shore of Gartan Lough. Gartan is a sublimely sweet and peaceful place, unlike the temperament of the saint celebrated there. Colmcille was a pious, holy and very learned man, and his influence was felt far and wide, but he was also fiery and hot-tempered, with an arrogance which no doubt arose from his aristocratic background and habit of authority. The traditional story of his exile to Iona is well known; it is regarded as 'the first copyright case'. He was a scholar, with a scholar's love of books, and this was long before Guthenberg and his printing press. Each 'book' had to be carefully and laboriously written out by hand, and naturally these manuscripts were much prized. St Finian of Moville had a manuscript which Colmcille coveted. When a request to copy it was refused (many of these early Irish saints weren't easy to live with), Colmcille copied it anyway, in secret. When Finian discovered the 'theft' he demanded that the copy be handed over to him. Colmcille refused. The case went to the High King for arbitration and he gave his famous verdict 'To every cow its calf, to every book its copy.' The consequent bad feelings arising between followers of the two holy men led to the Battle of Cuildrevne, and Colmcille, in sorrow and repentance, exiled himself to Iona, where he established his famous monastery which is still a renowned centre of retreat. The real explanation, however, is likely to have had more to do with some political tensions of the time in which Colmcille, with his background and temperament, became involved.

St Colmcille's Well, at Gartan, along with an ancient church and rudely-carved monastic boundary cross, is now marooned in a sea of tarmacadam which robs it of any atmosphere of sanctity. However, following the *turas* from numbered stations can help one to regain a sense of blessedness in this lovely area, where sheep graze and swans drift by Gartan's gentle shores. The ritual is quite a lengthy one and was given to me thus:

Doon Well, in County Donegal, is visited by thousands every year.

The stations of the turas are: 1 inside the little church, 2 the mound of stones behind the church, 3 the remains of a boundary cross behind the graveyard, 4 the ruins of the old abbey in the graveyard, 5 the boundary cross in front of the abbey, 6 approaching the holy well and 7 the well itself. At each station five Our Fathers, five Hail Marys, five Glorias and the Creed are said. Parts of the fifteen decades of the most holy Rosary are said between the stations, until all the decades are said. At stations 3, 4, 5 and 6 people walk round the first cross, the abbey ruins, the second cross and the well three times respectively and at the well, station 7, the water is lifted in a bottle. Part of the Rosary is recited while walking round the exterior wall of the graveyard between the stations.

There is no doubt that by the time this lengthy ritual is completed with its endless repetitions of prayers, a state of meditative calm and tranquillity would be arrived at. Call it holiness perhaps.

Away up in Fanad, where the road hugs the shore of Lough Swilly and the mountains of Inishowen are like smoke on the eastern horizon, a friend brought me to a Colmcille Well where, at first glance, one could think that the votive offerings of all the wells in Ireland had been gathered together. This is his description:

The wart well near Tarmon. To reach it means clambering about 7 metres (20 feet) up a rocky bank.

'Well-being'

If I just give you co-ordinates as: C240/423 Discovery Map 2, and directions as: About three kilometres or two miles out of Portsalon, County Donegal, on the Fanad Drive in the townland of Carryblough, you will think me the detached geographer reconstructing a digital landscape and you will not be touched.

If, however, I tell you that as a pair of landscape hunter-gatherers, we set out on a Saturday morning and totally unexpectedly bumped into this place of a magic roadside well, you may want to hear more. So I let Sean Healy from the first house down the road tell you and us, after an initial reaction of slight suspicion, 'For sure that's St Colmcille's Well. Always people come here and do the rounds and the pardon starts here on 9 June, Colum's feast day and lasts for a full nine days.'

And from behind him his utterly modern teenage daughter confirms the specifics of the 'pardon' (Pattern): 'three rounds of five Our Fathers by five Hail Marys by five

Glorias at each of the three stations around the cairn with a seven of the same at the well, always going with the sun of course; then take out your beads and say the rosary over three more rounds adding a stone to the pile each time round and finish off in front of the well. There leave your intention, with something.'

'Yes, yes' the father confirms 'she did it all for each of the nine days, and many more along with her. And there have been many, many cures.'

We are no longer the gawking tourists as we return to take in the scene once more. And our first incredulous look at the utterly mesmerising collection of objects spread over the well's covering stone or fluttering in the guardian hazel bush, transforms into a shudder of recognition of the width and depth of human suffering and failure: sure enough a baby's bib, but what about a faded bus ticket? And walking around again, we marvel at the height of the testimonial cairn and how a countless number of feet have contained the growth of summer to march out the trampled path of the round. And how a hand dip in the clear water holds an intimation of cleansing and 'well being'.

Fifty yards up the road we are led by another trail to a parallel well and meet Elizabeth McGinley who confides that weekly, besides her trip for groceries, she fills here two big containers with well water. For 'it's the only water for a proper cup of tea'.

And all of human life, the body in the soul, are fulfilled: well-being.

There are holy wells dedicated to Colmcille not only all over Donegal but all over Ireland, even in areas where there are no records to show that he ever visited. However, one of the most famous wells in Donegal is not at all connected with St Colmcille. It is Doon Well near Kilmacrenan, and its origin as a healing well is obscure. It appears to stretch back no farther than a few centuries at most, possibly to Famine times. According to a rather garbled account, it is associated with a certain 'Lector (teacher or professor) O'Friel', who was noted for his sanctity and his power as a healer, which attracted to him sufferers from all sorts of apparently incurable maladies. The 'Pilgrimage Souvenir' booklet tells us that:

… in his old age, when his vigour was waning and the shadow of death was hanging over him, his legion of clients became disturbed at the thought of losing such a holy and charitable man in whom God had implanted such power for miraculous healing. 'When I die my powers will live on after me' he assured them. Asked in what way such a wonderful thing would be possible, he told them that he would bless this Well at Doon and that those who drank or applied its water would have the benefit of his prayers of intercession.

There does not appear to be much other folklore, apart from another rather dubious story about how Lector O'Friel left his cane in Rome, but received a promise that wherever he found it, there he would also discover a well with mysterious powers, and that this is where he found it after eighteen visits.

For all the obscurity of its origins, it is held in great veneration right up to today, and thousands visit it every year, looking for cures for physical ailments and emotional or mental turmoil. The good lady of the house in which I stayed told me of a close relative of her own whose almost-blindness was cured by devotion to the well; another spoke about cancer. There is no set day for visiting Doon Well. People come at any time and rarely a day passes without a number of visitors. Up to a thousand people gather there on New Year's Eve and on May Eve, many carrying candles, some even now barefoot. 15 August, the feast of the Assumption of Our Lady, is also, as at so many wells, a special day. Traditionally one walked from home, no matter what the distance, in bare feet. The gatherings usually take on a festive atmosphere. In earlier decades trainloads of people came regularly from as far away as Derry.

I called on Mr and Mrs Gallagher on whose land the well is located — in fact, it is right outside their front door. They act as guardians, at much cost in both effort and finance. When I met her in the summer of 2000, Mary Gallagher was a handsome and gentle fresh-faced lady of middle years. She could not tell me much more than is written in the little booklet she sells there.

It presents a very different appearance nowadays from that seen in old photographs. With the co-operation of the Gallaghers, the well has been roofed in and surrounded with stone pathways. It now stands in the middle of a wide lawn alongside a large car park which is even equipped with toilets. Crutches and other objects seen in old photos decayed and passed into the bog before reclamation of the site, though some walking sticks are still embedded in the ground. Two young birch trees now stand near the well, quite festooned with the usual charms and votive offerings.

A stone marks the birthplace of Colmcille (Columba) at Gartan, County Donegal. The remains of Colmcille's monastery, another medieval church, two boundary crosses and the holy well are all within a short radius.

I asked Mary Gallagher if having such an important shrine right outside their door is not a big responsibility, but it is clear that she and her husband undertake the work and expense willingly (some small contributions can be made in a little box nearby by visitors who wish to do so). Down through the years, one of the family always had to be in attendance: visitors expected it. Compensation? No. But Mary Gallagher points to 'her own miracle'. This is her eleven children, all now grown, all healthy and successful, who never came to harm or danger from the crowds or hundreds of cars turning on her doorstep before renovation of the site and provision of a car park. She is satisfied.

There is more to Doon than the well. Close by is Carraig a' Dúin, the lofty rock on which the O'Donnells, chieftains of Tír Chonaill, were inaugurated. A plaque relates:

On this rock took place the secular ceremony of the inauguration of the O'Donnell Chieftains, the religious ceremony having taken place earlier in the nearby Abbey at Kilmacrenan.

Present were O'Friel (the inaugurator), the Bishop of Derry (successor of Colmcille), O'Cleary (the scribe) and chiefs, clergy and a host of others.

Twenty-five in all were inaugurated beginning with Eigneach, 1200 AD and ending with Niall Garbh 1603.

There is also a Mass Rock, one of those contrived altars where Mass was celebrated secretly in Penal times. It is well hidden, reached by a rough track through scrub and trees.

I mentioned my interest in Doon Well to my hosts near Kilmacrenan. Instantly, as in Athy, I was plied with names and legends of a dozen holy wells within striking distance. I was tired after a long day and just wanted to rest that evening, but telephone calls were made and I reluctantly heaved myself out of my armchair to meet up with yet another Mary Gallagher, to be brought to 'The Wart Well' not far away. This Wart Well proved to be worth the effort. It is seven or eight metres (twenty feet or more) up a rocky crag in the townland of Stradgraddy near the village of Tarmon. From below the only aid to locating it is by a white cross painted on the rock above it (by Mary Gallagher, who else?) which is visible from the road, if you know where to look. Even then you can lose sight of it while clambering up towards it.

It is indeed a strange and rather beautiful 'well' — in fact, it is not a well at all, but a

St Colmcille's Well, Fanad, County Donegal

heart-shaped bowl or depression in the rock, about half a metre (one-and-a-half feet) wide and about fifteen centimetres (six inches) deep. It is roofed over by a curved awning which echoes the curves of the bowl below, and the effect is of something deliberately and skilfully sculpted. It is difficult to see how it fills; locals suggest that the water comes up 'through the rock' and are adamant that it is not rain-water. It is not a spring, though there could perhaps be minute seepage through the crack dividing the bowl from the roof. There are odd votive objects left beside it — a few buttons, coins, holy pictures and a rosary, testifying to the fact that the well is still very much in use. 'Everyone comes here with their warts' I was told. 'Two of my own children had verrucas. At the clinic they treated them over a long period and made them even more painful. So I brought them to the well and from that day to this I haven't heard a word about them'. One woman claims to have been cured of cancer there. This being Colmcille country, the Wart Well is vaguely associated with the saint, but only vaguely, and as if out of politeness.

I describe this one not because it is important but just to indicate the vast variety of style and type of these places of faith and comfort.

Many wells have their guardians, sometimes hereditary, sometimes voluntary. An eye well in Donegal is one of the lucky ones, having young Pauric McGarvey to care for it. Aged nine he wrote in a local guidebook:[1]

The eye well is in Craig, Ray, Rathmullan. It is always full of water. It is a slab stone with a deep hollow in the centre. There is a little hole at the bottom of it where a spring comes up. It is the only eye well in the world. I don't know for how long it has been there. Often visitors come knocking on my door looking for information and facts about the eye well. I bring bottles of eye well

---

1. In *Walking Donegal — Rathmullan*, Derryveagh Glens Development Association.

water to my relations in Scotland. The eye doctors think that it cured my friend. This is a story that my Granny told me. One day a boy called Anderson was hired by my Mammy's Granny to herd some cows in the field where the eye well was. He started kicking some stones in the well and blocked it up. So that day he went home and got his supper and told his mother what he had done and went to bed. The next morning the young boy was blind. He could not see a thing. He gave his Mum a fright. The boy ran through six fields to get to the eye well.

His Mum said 'Now this is what you have to do. Take out all the stones, like a good boy.' Every stone he took out his eyesight came back bit by bit. Then the boy took back everything he had done. The next day he was better and went to work again. I take care of the well and I love when people come enquiring about it.

Pauric had cleared the grass and nettles from around the well and decorated it 'with nice white stones'. He had chosen quartz, the sacred stone, purely by instinct.

12

Maumeen

The track up the mountainside was rough and stony, and the gale lashing the rain into our faces made it difficult to watch our footsteps among the mud and rocks.

It was July, but it was a wild and wintry day. People struggled up the mountainside from both directions, some to shelter under rocks or huddle around the little chapel where the priest was hearing Confessions. One by one they entered, told their sins and were absolved, to step back out into the rain, no doubt feeling lighter. While this was in progress, other groups were making the traditional Stations. This involved walking seven times around each of the two Beds (old circles of stones) and St Patrick's Well, reciting the Our Father, Hail Mary and the Glory at each round: ancient circlings, magic numbers. To complete the traditional Station, the pilgrim advanced to Leaba Phádraig (St Patrick's Bed) to ask for the intercession of St Patrick for grace or favours. When Confessions were completed the priest emerged and, preceded by a

Priest and pilgrims on Maumeen, 'the Pass of the Birds', follow the Stations of the Cross on the mountainside.

Brother in a white smock holding a large Cross, the Christian 'Stations of the Cross' began. Backwards and forwards, zigzagging through the boulders, slipping and stumbling over wet rocks and steep heather, a procession formed behind the celebrant, moving from Station to Station, prayers and hymns snatched by the gale, the priest's white shock of hair shining like a halo above his white surplice, the cross held aloft at the head of the procession, the scene taking on extraordinary drama in that already dramatic setting. Fourteen stations in all, prayers and a hymn for each as thunder rumbled overhead. Then Mass was celebrated in the tiny chapel, the priest inside, the congregation outside.

After that, individually to the well, for older rituals, and to collect water to help healing through the year to come. Gradually, pilgrims drifted back down the mountainside as a weak ray of sunshine broke through the clouds. As we descended people spoke of the previous year, assuring me I would have been 'scalded by the sun'.

Maumeen is Maam Éan, the Pass of the Birds, and it is indeed an airy place, a high and rugged pass through the Maamturk (Pass of the Boar) mountains in Connemara. At the summit of the pass is St Patrick's Well and a cleft in the rock known as St Patrick's Bed. Long before Patrick, however, this had been the location of one of the great Lughnasa festivals. In common with many other festivals it was Christianised and associated with St Patrick, but retained its links with the past by continuing to hold its great Pattern on Garland Sunday, the last Sunday of July (or, sometimes, the first Sunday of August). The occasion had ceased until revived in the 1980s with a new set of devotional observances. A

A pilgrim at the well.

Opposite page and page 99: A modern statue of the saint as shepherd stands on the mountain pass, in front of the pilgrimage altar'.

small chapel was constructed clinging to the escarpment, and stone crosses were set up to mark the Stations of the Cross, crossing and re-crossing the pathways of the old 'stations' which people still circled, using pebbles to count their rounds. Apart from its efficacy in healing human ills, the well water is used to cure murrain in cattle. The site of the well has been relocated higher up the mountainside (following the spring) for reasons, apparently, of hygiene, but people tend nonetheless to be drawn to the old well site, which is still there and which shows more signs of devotion in terms of a small collection of votive offerings.

The people from Connemara, to the west of Maumeen, and the people of Joyce Country to the east, both claimed hegemony of the well. They used to hold their Pattern on the same day and on the same ground, but slightly apart, and the day usually ended in what would have been regarded as 'a grand fight', the women piling up stones for their men to use as ammunition.

13

From Mullagh to Würzburg

From the very local to the international. The city of Würzburg is one of the jewels of Germany's 'Romantic Road'. It is in the heart of Germany's Rosinenland, and famous for its Baroque grandeur. Its marvellous buildings include the imposing Neumünster and the Dom, the interior of which is described as 'a shimmering rococo treasure house'.

In June 2000, the famous Cathedral Choir of Würzburg, accompanied by the Auxiliary Bishop of that Diocese, travelled to the small, quiet town of Mullagh in County Cavan to perform a concert in Mullagh's little Parish Church.

What, you may well ask, did Mullagh do to deserve such a signal honour? What it did was to give birth to the patron saint of Würzburg, our St Kilian.

Kilian was born about the year 640 in the townland of Cloughballybeg near Mullagh, twelve kilometres (eight miles) north of Kells. In the style of many Irish monks of the time, Kilian decided to become 'an exile for

Christ' and set sail for the Continent from Kilmackilloge harbour near Kenmare in County Kerry in the year 686. He made his way along the rivers Rhine and Main into Franconia where, tradition tells us, he planted a cross on the Krenzberg hill overlooking what is now the city of Würzburg. Here he commenced his missionary activities, succeeding in baptising thousands of converts. Among them was Gosbert, duke of the local territory. In order to be baptised, however, Kilian insisted that Gosbert put aside his wife, who was his brother's widow. The enraged woman arranged to have Kilian and his two companions, Colonat and Totnan, assassinated. Remains of the three martyrs are now enshrined in a richly elaborate reliquary. Each year on Kilian's feastday, 8 July, the shrine is carried in solemn procession through the streets of Würzburg as part of the Kilianfest, one of the best known festivals of the German people, and is exhibited in the Cathedral, the Cathedral of St Kilian, during the octave.

The Well of St Kilian of Würzburg, near Mullagh, County Cavan.

The shrine is very beautiful. A bronze framework houses seventy-two squares of rock crystal through which the skulls, adorned with precious stones, can actually be seen.

This all seems a long way from Mullagh, and still more from Cloughballybeg where St Kilian's Holy Well is located. The well, or spring, is next to Longfield Bridge about four kilometres (three miles) beyond Mullagh on the Virginia Road. It is contained by a wall of rough stones, surrounded by a whitethorn hedge. A cross is built into the surrounding stonework and a small statue of the saint stands above. A sign gives the information:

The relics of St Kilian and his two martyred companions can be seen inside the crystal walls of the reliquary.

By kind permission of the St Kilian Heritage Centre, Mullagh, County Cavan

Holy Well and Birthplace of St Kilian.
*   Born 640 AD.*
And Ordained at Roscarbery, Co Cork.
*   Founded Monastery at*
Tuosist, Co Kerry. Arrived Würzburg
*   W. Germany in 686 AD.*
Martyred in Würzburg 689 AD. Feast day
*   8 July.*

St Kilian's shrine is carried through the streets of Würzburg during the annual pilgrimage.
By kind permission of the St Kilian Heritage Centre, Mullagh, County Cavan

As are so many of these blessed wells, it is in a lovely area, and the nearby lake with its reeds and water lilies offers an idyllic spot for a picnic.

It was customary for pilgrims to gather at the well on the eve of the feastday to do the usual rounds, the rituals ending with socialising and merrymaking. Despite occasional attempts to stop the practice in the eighteenth and nineteenth centuries, the well is still venerated but people come individually now rather than in large gatherings, both on 8 July and at other times.

It is a nice thought that as the citizens of Würzburg, the high, the mighty and the humble devout, follow the magnificent casket containing the relics of their patron as it is borne through the streets of that city, the people who live in Mullagh and surrounding area, who come to kneel quietly on the rough stones to pray and sip the water at St Kilian's Well, are honouring the same man, but the people of Cloughballybeg can claim him as their own.

A Heritage Centre dedicated to the saint has been built by the local community in Mullagh, in association with the Diocese of Würzburg which donated an Exhibition and relics. It is an unpretentious stone-faced building with an audio visual display and a café. Exhibits include a copy of the Codex of the life and martyrdom of Kilian which was published some time between the eighth and tenth centuries. It contains a sequence of illustrations which are probably the oldest detailed illustrations of any saint's life.

Cover of a codex in the University Library in Würzburg, which illustrates the murder of St Kilian and his two companions and the elevation of their souls to heaven.
By kind permission of the owners, the University Library of Würzburg

14

Some Island Wells

I can never cross the sandbar to Omey Island without hearing the poem echo in my mind: 'O Mary, call the cattle home, across the sands of Dee.' Poor Mary, of course, met a watery end, but great carelessness would be needed to meet such a fate on the way to or from Omey.

Omey is one of several quasi-islands on the tattered western fringe of Connemara. The sea advances and retreats across a wide causeway, allowing approach on foot courtesy of a lunar timetable. It can be driven across also, but somehow the walk across the sand prepares one for the state of mind that an island both induces and deserves. Even in terms of Connemara, where the twentieth century has only a marginal grip, crossing the sands to Omey is entering another world. The island is almost entirely composed of duach, grass-grown sand. A single sandy road meanders about halfway through it, after which a 'green road' winds around a lake towards the other end of the island. There is a scattering of houses, some of which are holiday homes, others maintained though not normally lived in by islanders living elsewhere. In the year 2000, it had a single permanent inhabitant.

Omey is roughly circular, about a mile in diameter, with a bay, Trá Rabhach, on the western side and a little promontory on the north-western corner, above Trá na nÉan, the Strand of the Birds. The old name for the island was Iomaidh Feichin, or St Feichin's Seat, and the lake which occupies the centre of the island is Feichin's Lake.

Feichin is the founder of the famous monastic settlement of Fore in County

Westmeath (see Chapter 9). He died in the year 664 of the Yellow Plague which devastated the country at that time. He came to Omey because:

... an angel appeared to Feichin in his sleep and said to him: 'The inhabitants of the island named Imaid (Omey), and the rest of the people of that country, are in darkness as to the divine law; and get thee to preach to them. For God hath granted to thee their tribute and their due, and it is thou who shall be unto them a lord and counsellor and bush of protection and judge of doom'. At the angel's command Feichin went into the west of Connaught to Imaid, and he blessed it, and built a cloister therein, and brought those tribes under a yoke of belief and piety, and baptised them in a well which brake forth for him from the ground through the miracles of God and the powers of Feichin.

Remnants of his cloister — or, rather, of a later building on the site — are almost buried in the drifting sand. The holy well (could it be the same one 'which brake forth for him from the ground' all those centuries ago?) is still visited regularly. It is on the western shoreline close to where rocks run in a smooth flow down to the sea and some distance from the monastic remains, which are towards the north. It is a small pothole in the grass, surrounded generously by a curved stone-built wall. The water trickles out onto the rocks below it and it was from here that people collected water in bottles to take away. In August 2000 some tokens had been left on a broad slab above the opening, showing that it had not been abandoned.

From the tip of Omey the endless complexity of this part of Connemara displays itself. Land and sea, island and lake

---

Opposite page: St Feichin's Well on Omey Island which, according to the Annals, 'brake forth for him from the ground through the miracles of God and the powers of Feichin'.

Cruagh Island as seen from St Feichin's Well on Omey Island.

seem to be inextricably intertwined, while the jagged outline of Cruagh Island glimmers on the western horizon. As I wandered towards the monastery I met up with a young couple who were taking their ease on a rock, he a fine vigorous-looking young man, she fresh-faced and smiling, blonde curls blowing across her face. We greeted each other and fell into chat. He told me that he and his wife lived now on the nearby mainland, but he belonged to the last family to have left the island. Jobs on the mainland didn't adapt themselves to the comings and goings of the tide.

He and his five siblings had been the last at the island school as the number of families dwindled. When there were only four of them left, the roof of the school fell in. His father moved desks from the school to the house and made a classroom of one of his few rooms. When the oldest left, leaving only three, the Department wouldn't supply a teacher, and that was the end of schooling on the island.

His father took a house on the mainland, but in common with most of the other island families, he retained the old home, visiting regularly to light fires and keep the house in repair, or perhaps keeping a few animals and spending the occasional holiday there. He spoke of his grandfather's ten sons, nine of whom emigrated to America, leaving only his father in the old home. I asked him whether they had children of their own. 'We're expecting our first today' was his startling reply, and they looked at each other and laughed. I hadn't noticed she was so thoroughly 'with child'. We parted, and I watched them wander off serenely, hand in hand, towards the holy well. 'Fertility, of course,' I thought — here of all places, where life is regulated by the lunar cycle.

Another of these western islands (a real island this time) is Inishlackan, the Island of the Flagstones, also beautiful, also un-inhabited except for some inoffensive holiday retreats. It also has its holy well to which is attributed healing properties, though this is

Our Lady's Island, County Wexford. It has been a celebrated place of pilgrimage for several centuries.

one of a type not uncommon around the coast, not just here on the western seaboard but in all coastal areas. It is really a circular depression in the rocks at high-tide mark, that holds fresh water except when inundated by the sea. Rainwater, one presumes, but folklore insists that they never go dry and that the water is always fresh. The well at Inishlackan is a particularly difficult one to find and after much searching I eventually had to ask for help. It is also an especially modest one, very small and sheltered by a rock shelf on the southern shore. There are no identifying marks. Only when you discover its location do you notice the faintly smoothened track across the rocks towards it. Inishlackan appears to have only one true well to serve its inhabitants, and that itself is below high-tide mark. In the past, fetching water meant waiting for the tide to ebb and the fresh water to bubble up again. Strangely, this was not thought to be at all miraculous. Nowadays water is pumped to a holding tank in the centre of the island.

Then there is Inishnee, which is reached by a bridge from the mainland near Roundstone. St Colmcille's Well on that island is on the northern shore, a short distance from the bridge and not too easily approached. It is a perfectly round depression in the rock, about thirty centimetres across and sixty centimetres deep (one foot across and two foot deep). There is another smaller opening a short distance to the west of it. Both are marked by shoulder-high cairns of stones which can normally be seen from the road, but which get knocked down from time to time by the tide, and are rebuilt by the owner of the adjoining land, one John King when I visited it in 1998. The traditional pattern day was St Colmcille's Day, 9 June, and whereas no pattern takes place nowadays, it is still occasionally visited quietly by individuals. Tokens, including coins, are sometimes left. Rounds are made, with prayers, of both cairns.

There are two similar wells at Mweenish near Carna and no doubt others that I haven't discovered. And please God I never will: I don't want ever to exhaust my excuse for poking around among the rocks and pools and headlands.

the latest. The island presents a lovely green sward sweeping into the lagoon where swans drift and gather. It is obviously a popular place for strolling and picnicking, but you

Inishlackan's tiny 'holy well'.

Something of a very different nature is Our Lady's Island in County Wexford, with its renowned pilgrimage tradition.

It is a large low-lying island in a saltwater lagoon called, appropriately, Lough Tocair — the Lake of the Causeway. The Causeway is thought to date back to pre-Norman times at

can imagine a wild gale coming across it on any day of the year. A large number of raths or ring-forts offer evidence that it was densely inhabited in very early times and in medieval days a castle was built to guard the causeway. There are also ruins of a small church. The earliest name of the island was

Cluain-na-mBan, the Meadow of the Women. Two famous shrines of sun worship are known to have existed in this locality, one at a very large rath enclosure at Ballytrent, the other at Carnsore Point, where there is also a holy well, so it appears likely that the women of the title were druidesses. It seems that the old cult was Christianised with the coming of St Abban, the druidic dedication switched to the Blessed Virgin, and the pilgrimage tradition of today, which involves a circumnavigation of the island, is probably a continuation or, at least, a revival of one already established by then.

Today's pilgrimage, which could be said to have national status, is indeed a fine affair. A large glass-walled shrine is provided for religious ceremonies. Individuals and small groups make the round of the island at any time, and especially on 15 August, but the principal event takes place on the evening of 8 September, the feast of the Nativity of our Lady. A torchlight procession of many hundreds, sometimes thousands, of pilgrims winds its way around the island; prayers are intoned, hymns sung and Mass celebrated. It is all very impressive, especially as 'stations' are laid out along the route, with benches where weary pilgrims can rest before continuing their penitential journey. But sheltering shyly under the embankment on the western side of the island, as if intimidated by all this power and glory, is the small holy well which, for all we know, was used by the original eponymous Women. It is the recipient of the prayers and requests — and probably thanksgivings — of a quieter and more private kind than the larger pilgrimage. Little offerings rest on the ledge: scapulars, medals, a holy picture or two, a small statue, now broken, of the Blessed Virgin. It is a very moving manifestation of the endurance of old forms alongside the newer dispensation.

15

Saving the Wells

There are other ways of being miraculous. To me, the most magical of all island wells is the one that served the monks in that most isolated and extreme of settlements, the monastery perched dizzyingly on the summit of Skellig Michael, a spike of rock rearing up 220 metres (700 foot) out of the Atlantic, twelve kilometres (nine miles) off the Kerry coast. Though it is not known as a holy well, what could be more miraculous than the small stone basin that manages to hold sweet water winter and summer in that wind and spray-swept haunt of puffins and storm petrels? It is difficult for modern minds to grapple with the fearful simplicity of the lives of the monks who chose that spot so close to the heavens. And the heavens provided them with constant sweet water in that impossible place. It appears that if we have faith enough, our needs are fulfilled.

The offerings left at wells seem to reflect every need of human existence: for health, for fertility, for jobs, for houses, for a good partner in life, for family harmony. The coming to the well, especially if that entails

some hardship, the circling of the 'stations', the adding of stones to cairns, the prayers repeated like a mantra, all of these serve to focus the mind to a degree that allows our own healing powers to come into play, or at least to bring peace to mind and soul.

The holy wells have survived, despite the lack of any official help or protection. They have always belonged to the people, the ordinary folk of the countryside who have no office, power, or influence. They were denounced by both Church and State during the eighteenth and nineteenth centuries, by the Church as being idolatrous superstition, by the State as being occasions of disorderly behaviour. Yet the people remained faithful to their local gods or saints and their sacred wells in the face of threats of fines and whippings or eternal damnation.

Many of the wells today are maintained by local lay community groups. In recent years the Churches in some parishes have begun to re-evaluate them as the focus of genuine piety, and to incorporate visits and prayers at the wells as part of their own Christian feast-day rituals.

The cult of the wells could not have endured so long unless it satisfied some deep-felt need in our consciousness, and it would be a great shame to let it die out. As mentioned already, there is scarcely a townland in Ireland that does not have at least one holy well that deserves attention. Looking at the practice at its most mundane level, a visit to the well offers a pleasant excursion. Usually the place is picturesque and worth visiting for its own sake. Once there, it seems a simple exercise of customary form to carry out the prescribed rituals, and have the satisfaction of knowing we have participated in a ceremony that connects us to our deepest and oldest roots.

Opposite page: In the background is Teampaill Finghín and the round tower at Clonmacnois. In the foreground, all that is left of what was once a well dedicated to St Finghín (St Finian).

References

Anderson and Ogilvie (eds), *Adomnan: Life of Columba*, London: 1961.

Bradley, Richard, *An Archaeology of Natural Places*, London: 2000.

Brenneman, Walter L., Jr, and Mary G: *Crossing the Circle at the Holy Wells of Ireland*, Virginia: 1995.

Cambrensis, Giraldus, *The History and Topography of Ireland*, trans. John J. O'Meara, London: 1982.

Connolly, Susan, and Moroney, Anne-Marie,: *Stone and Tree Sheltering Water – An Exploration of Sacred and Secular Wells in County Louth*.

Corkery, Rev. John, *Saint Manchan and his Shrine*, Maynooth: 1970.

Dames, Michael, *Mythic Ireland*, Thames & Hudson, 1992.

Danaher, Kevin, *The Holy Wells of Co. Dublin*, Archiv. Hib. Vol 2.

Danaher, Kevin, *The Holy Wells of Corkaguiney, Co. Kerry*, JRSAI, 1960.

Gibson, Alex, *Circles and Henges: reincarnations of past traditions?* Archaeology Ireland, 2000.

Harbison, Peter, *Pilgrimage in Ireland*, London: 1991.

Harbison, Peter, *Guide to the National Monuments of Ireland*, Dublin: 1970.

Hardy, Philip Dixon, *The Holy Wells of Ireland*, Dublin: 1836.

Herity, Michael, *Gleanncholmcille*, Glencolmcille: 1990.

History of St. Brigid's Church, Blanchardstown 1837–1987, pub by the Parish.

Inglis, Tom, *Moral Monopoly The Rise and Fall of the Catholic Church in Modern Ireland*, University College Dublin Press.

Joyce, Weston St John, *The Neighbourhood of Dublin*, Dublin: 1912.

Killanin, Lord, and Duignan, Michael V., *The Shell Guide to Ireland*, London: 1962.

Lavelle, Des, *Skellig, Island Outpost of Europe*, Dublin: 1976.

Logan, Patrick, *The Holy Wells of Ireland*, Colin Smythe, 1980.

MacNeill, Máire, *The Festival of Lughnasa*, Oxford: 1962

Minehan, Rita, CSB, *Rekindling the Flame A Pilgrimage in the Footsteps of Brigid of Kildare*.

Murphy, W., *The Pattern of Mullinakill*, Old Kilkenny Review, 1970.

Ó hÓgáin, Daithí, *Myth, Legend & Romance*, Prentice Hall, 1991.

O'Farrell, Padraic, *Fore – The Fact and The Fantasy*, Mullingar: 1984.

O'Flaherty, Roderick, *A Chorographical Description of h-Iar Connaught*, Dublin: 1846.

Our Lady's Island Rosary Pilgrimage.

Plummer, Charles, *Lives of Irish Saints*, Oxford: 1922.

Pochin Mould, Daphne, *Irish Pilgrimage*, Dublin: 1955.

Purcell, Deirdre, *On Lough Derg*, Veritas, Dublin: 1988.

Robinson, *Stones of Aran. Labyrinth*, Dublin: 1995.

Sharkey, Olive, *Fore and its Ancient Buildings*, Mullingar: 1999.

Stokes, Whitley, *Lives of Saints from the Book of Lismore*, Oxford: 1890.

Synge, J.M., *The Aran Islands*, London and Dublin: 1907.

Synge, J.M., *The Well of the Saints*, London and New York: 1905.

Tochar Phadraig, *A Pilgrim's Progress: Ballintubber Abbey*.

Uí Dháiligh, Eilis, *Saint Gobnait of Ballyvourney*.

Walking Donegal – Rathmullan, Derryveagh Glens Development Association.

Weir, Anthony, *Early Ireland, A Field Guide*, Blackstaff Press, 1980.

Yeats, W.B., *At the Hawk's Well: Collected Plays*, London. 1955.

Index